KLEMENS
VON
METTERNICH

KLEMENS VON METTERNICH

John von der Heide

CHELSEA HOUSE PUBLISHERS
NEW YORK
NEW HAVEN   PHILADELPHIA

EDITOR-IN-CHIEF: Nancy Toff
EXECUTIVE EDITOR: Remmel T. Nunn
MANAGING EDITOR: Karyn Gullen Browne
COPY CHIEF: Juliann Barbato
PICTURE EDITOR: Adrian G. Allen
ART DIRECTOR: Giannella Garrett
MANUFACTURING MANAGER: Gerald Levine

Staff for KLEMENS VON METTERNICH:

SENIOR EDITOR: John W. Selfridge
ASSISTANT EDITOR: Bert Yaeger
COPY EDITOR: Ellen Scordato
EDITORIAL ASSISTANT: Sean Ginty
ASSOCIATE PICTURE EDITOR: Juliette Dickstein
PICTURE RESEARCHER: Elie Porter
SENIOR DESIGNER: Debbie Jay
ASSISTANT DESIGNER: Jill Goldreyer
PRODUCTION COORDINATOR: Joseph Romano
COVER ILLUSTRATION: Michael Mariano

CREATIVE DIRECTOR: Harold Steinberg

First Printing

1 3 5 7 9 8 6 4 2

Library of Congress Cataloging in Publication Data

Von der Heide, John T. METTERNICH.

(World leaders past and present)
Bibliography: p.
Includes index.
1. Metternich, Clemens Wenzel Lothar, Fürst von,
1773–1859. 2. Statesman—Austria—Biography.
3. Austria—Foreign relations—1792–1835. 4. Europe—
Politics and government—1789–1915. 5. Europe—Politics
and government—1815–1848. I. Title. II. Series: World
leaders past & present.
DB80.8.M57V66   1988   940.2′7′0924 [B] 87-25609

ISBN 0-87754-541-3

Contents

John Adams
John Quincy Adams
Konrad Adenauer
Alexander the Great
Salvador Allende
Marc Antony
Corazon Aquino
Yasir Arafat
King Arthur
Hafez al-Assad
Kemal Atatürk
Attila
Clement Attlee
Augustus Caesar
Menachem Begin
David Ben-Gurion
Otto von Bismarck
Léon Blum
Simon Bolívar
Cesare Borgia
Willy Brandt
Leonid Brezhnev
Julius Caesar
John Calvin
Jimmy Carter
Fidel Castro
Catherine the Great
Charlemagne
Chiang Kai-Shek
Winston Churchill
Georges Clemenceau
Cleopatra
Constantine the Great
Hernán Cortés
Oliver Cromwell
Georges-Jacques
    Danton
Jefferson Davis
Moshe Dayan
Charles de Gaulle
Eamon De Valera
Eugene Debs
Deng Xiaoping
Benjamin Disraeli
Alexander Dubček
François & Jean-Claude
    Duvalier
Dwight Eisenhower
Eleanor of Aquitaine
Elizabeth i
Faisal
Ferdinand & Isabella
Francisco Franco
Benjamin Franklin

Frederick the Great
Indira Gandhi
Mohandas Gandhi
Giuseppe Garibaldi
Amin & Bashir Gemayel
Genghis Khan
William Gladstone
Mikhail Gorbachev
Ulysses S. Grant
Ernesto "Che" Guevara
Tenzin Gyatso
Alexander Hamilton
Dag Hammarskjöld
Henry viii
Henry of Navarre
Paul von Hindenburg
Hirohito
Adolf Hitler
Ho Chi Minh
King Hussein
Ivan the Terrible
Andrew Jackson
James i
Wojciech Jaruzelski
Thomas Jefferson
Joan of Arc
Pope John xxiii
Pope John Paul ii
Lyndon Johnson
Benito Juárez
John Kennedy
Robert Kennedy
Jomo Kenyatta
Ayatollah Khomeini
Nikita Khrushchev
Kim Il Sung
Martin Luther King, Jr.
Henry Kissinger
Kublai Khan
Lafayette
Robert E. Lee
Vladimir Lenin
Abraham Lincoln
David Lloyd George
Louis xiv
Martin Luther
Judas Maccabeus
James Madison
Nelson & Winnie
    Mandela
Mao Zedong
Ferdinand Marcos
George Marshall

Mary, Queen of Scots
Tomáš Masaryk
Golda Meir
Klemens von Metternich
James Monroe
Hosni Mubarak
Robert Mugabe
Benito Mussolini
Napoléon Bonaparte
Gamal Abdel Nasser
Jawaharlal Nehru
Nero
Nicholas II
Richard Nixon
Kwame Nkrumah
Daniel Ortega
Mohammed Reza Pahlavi
Thomas Paine
Charles Stewart
    Parnell
Pericles
Juan Perón
Peter the Great
Pol Pot
Muammar el-Qaddafi
Ronald Reagan
Cardinal Richelieu
Maximilien Robespierre
Eleanor Roosevelt
Franklin Roosevelt
Theodore Roosevelt
Anwar Sadat
Haile Selassie
Prince Sihanouk
Jan Smuts
Joseph Stalin
Sukarno
Sun Yat-sen
Tamerlane
Mother Teresa
Margaret Thatcher
Josip Broz Tito
Toussaint L'Ouverture
Leon Trotsky
Pierre Trudeau
Harry Truman
Queen Victoria
Lech Walesa
George Washington
Chaim Weizmann
Woodrow Wilson
Xerxes
Emiliano Zapata
Zhou Enlai

CHELSEA HOUSE PUBLISHERS

ON LEADERSHIP

Arthur M. Schlesinger, jr.

LEADERSHIP, it may be said, is really what makes the world go round. Love no doubt smooths the passage; but love is a private transaction between consenting adults. Leadership is a public transaction with history. The idea of leadership affirms the capacity of individuals to move, inspire, and mobilize masses of people so that they act together in pursuit of an end. Sometimes leadership serves good purposes, sometimes bad; but whether the end is benign or evil, great leaders are those men and women who leave their personal stamp on history.

Now, the very concept of leadership implies the proposition that individuals can make a difference. This proposition has never been universally accepted. From classical times to the present day, eminent thinkers have regarded individuals as no more than the agents and pawns of larger forces, whether the gods and goddesses of the ancient world or, in the modern era, race, class, nation, the dialectic, the will of the people, the spirit of the times, history itself. Against such forces, the individual dwindles into insignificance.

So contends the thesis of historical determinism. Tolstoy's great novel *War and Peace* offers a famous statement of the case. Why, Tolstoy asked, did millions of men in the Napoleonic Wars, denying their human feelings and their common sense, move back and forth across Europe slaughtering their fellows? "The war," Tolstoy answered, "was bound to happen simply because it was bound to happen." All prior history predetermined it. As for leaders, they, Tolstoy said, "are but the labels that serve to give a name to an end and, like labels, they have the least possible connection with the event." The greater the leader, "the more conspicuous the inevitability and the predestination of every act he commits." The leader, said Tolstoy, is "the slave of history."

Determinism takes many forms. Marxism is the determinism of class. Nazism the determinism of race. But the idea of men and women as the slaves of history runs athwart the deepest human instincts. Rigid determinism abolishes the idea of human freedom—

7

the assumption of free choice that underlies every move we make, every word we speak, every thought we think. It abolishes the idea of human responsibility, since it is manifestly unfair to reward or punish people for actions that are by definition beyond their control. No one can live consistently by any deterministic creed. The Marxist states prove this themselves by their extreme susceptibility to the cult of leadership.

More than that, history refutes the idea that individuals make no difference. In December 1931 a British politician crossing Park Avenue in New York City between 76th and 77th Streets around 10:30 P.M. looked in the wrong direction and was knocked down by an automobile—a moment, he later recalled, of a man aghast, a world aglare: "I do not understand why I was not broken like an eggshell or squashed like a gooseberry." Fourteen months later an American politician, sitting in an open car in Miami, Florida, was fired on by an assassin; the man beside him was hit. Those who believe that individuals make no difference to history might well ponder whether the next two decades would have been the same had Mario Constasino's car killed Winston Churchill in 1931 and Giuseppe Zangara's bullet killed Franklin Roosevelt in 1933. Suppose, in addition, that Adolf Hitler had been killed in the street fighting during the Munich *Putsch* of 1923 and that Lenin had died of typhus during World War I. What would the 20th century be like now?

For better or for worse, individuals do make a difference. "The notion that a people can run itself and its affairs anonymously," wrote the philosopher William James, "is now well known to be the silliest of absurdities. Mankind does nothing save through initiatives on the part of inventors, great or small, and imitation by the rest of us—these are the sole factors in human progress. Individuals of genius show the way, and set the patterns, which common people then adopt and follow."

Leadership, James suggests, means leadership in thought as well as in action. In the long run, leaders in thought may well make the greater difference to the world. But, as Woodrow Wilson once said, "Those only are leaders of men, in the general eye, who lead in action. . . . It is at their hands that new thought gets its translation into the crude language of deeds." Leaders in thought often invent in solitude and obscurity, leaving to later generations the tasks of imitation. Leaders in action—the leaders portrayed in this series—have to be effective in their own time.

And they cannot be effective by themselves. They must act in response to the rhythms of their age. Their genius must be adapted, in a phrase of William James's, "to the receptivities of the moment." Leaders are useless without followers. "There goes the mob," said the French politician hearing a clamor in the streets. "I am their leader. I must follow them." Great leaders turn the inchoate emotions of the mob to purposes of their own. They seize on the opportunities of their time, the hopes, fears, frustrations, crises, potentialities. They succeed when events have prepared the way for them, when the community is awaiting to be aroused, when they can provide the clarifying and organizing ideas. Leadership ignites the circuit between the individual and the mass and thereby alters history.

It may alter history for better or for worse. Leaders have been responsible for the most extravagant follies and most monstrous crimes that have beset suffering humanity. They have also been vital in such gains as humanity has made in individual freedom, religious and racial tolerance, social justice, and respect for human rights.

There is no sure way to tell in advance who is going to lead for good and who for evil. But a glance at the gallery of men and women in *World Leaders—Past and Present* suggests some useful tests.

One test is this: Do leaders lead by force or by persuasion? By command or by consent? Through most of history leadership was exercised by the divine right of authority. The duty of followers was to defer and to obey. "Theirs not to reason why / Theirs but to do and die." On occasion, as with the so-called enlightened despots of the 18th century in Europe, absolutist leadership was animated by humane purposes. More often, absolutism nourished the passion for domination, land, gold, and conquest and resulted in tyranny.

The great revolution of modern times has been the revolution of equality. The idea that all people should be equal in their legal condition has undermined the old structure of authority, hierarchy, and deference. The revolution of equality has had two contrary effects on the nature of leadership. For equality, as Alexis de Tocqueville pointed out in his great study *Democracy in America*, might mean equality in servitude as well as equality in freedom.

"I know of only two methods of establishing equality in the political world," Tocqueville wrote. "Rights must be given to every citizen, or none at all to anyone . . . save one, who is the master of all." There was no middle ground "between the sovereignty of all and the absolute power of one man." In his astonishing prediction of 20th-century totalitarian dictatorship, Tocqueville explained how the revolution of equality could lead to the *"Führerprinzip"* and more terrible absolutism than the world had ever known.

But when rights are given to every citizen and the sovereignty of all is established, the problem of leadership takes a new form, becomes more exacting than ever before. It is easy to issue commands and enforce them by the rope and the stake, the concentration camp and the *gulag.* It is much harder to use argument and achievement to overcome opposition and win consent. The Founding Fathers of the United States understood the difficulty. They believed that history had given them the opportunity to decide, as Alexander Hamilton wrote in the first Federalist Paper, whether men are indeed capable of basing government on "reflection and choice, or whether they are forever destined to depend . . . on accident and force."

Government by reflection and choice called for a new style of leadership and a new quality of followership. It required leaders to be responsive to popular concerns, and it required followers to be active and informed participants in the process. Democracy does not eliminate emotion from politics; sometimes it fosters demagoguery; but it is confident that, as the greatest of democratic leaders put it, you cannot fool all of the people all of the time. It measures leadership by results and retires those who overreach or falter or fail.

It is true that in the long run despots are measured by results too. But they can postpone the day of judgment, sometimes indefinitely, and in the meantime they can do infinite harm. It is also true that democracy is no guarantee of virtue and intelligence in government, for the voice of the people is not necessarily the voice of God. But democracy, by assuring the right of opposition, offers built-in resistance to the evils inherent in absolutism. As the theologian Reinhold Niebuhr summed it up, "Man's capacity for justice makes democracy possible, but man's inclination to injustice makes democracy necessary."

A second test for leadership is the end for which power is sought. When leaders have as their goal the supremacy of a master race or the promotion of totalitarian revolution or the acquisition and exploitation of colonies or the protection of greed and privilege or the preservation of personal power, it is likely that their leadership will do little to advance the cause of humanity. When their goal is the abolition of slavery, the liberation of women, the enlargement of opportunity for the poor and powerless, the extension of equal rights to racial minorities, the defense of the freedoms of expression and opposition, it is likely that their leadership will increase the sum of human liberty and welfare.

Leaders have done great harm to the world. They have also conferred great benefits. You will find both sorts in this series. Even "good" leaders must be regarded with a certain wariness. Leaders are not demigods; they put on their trousers one leg after another just like ordinary mortals. No leader is infallible, and every leader needs to be reminded of this at regular intervals. Irreverence irritates leaders but is their salvation. Unquestioning submission corrupts leaders and demeans followers. Making a cult of a leader is always a mistake. Fortunately hero worship generates its own antidote. "Every hero," said Emerson, "becomes a bore at last."

The signal benefit the great leaders confer is to embolden the rest of us to live according to our own best selves, to be active, insistent, and resolute in affirming our own sense of things. For great leaders attest to the reality of human freedom against the supposed inevitabilities of history. And they attest to the wisdom and power that may lie within the most unlikely of us, which is why Abraham Lincoln remains the supreme example of great leadership. A great leader, said Emerson, exhibits new possibilities to all humanity. "We feed on genius. . . . Great men exist that there may be greater men."

Great leaders, in short, justify themselves by emancipating and empowering their followers. So humanity struggles to master its destiny, remembering with Alexis de Tocqueville: "It is true that around every man a fatal circle is traced beyond which he cannot pass; but within the wide verge of that circle he is powerful and free; as it is with man, so with communities."

1

The Just Equilibrium

In the British Museum there is a print depicting the Congress of Vienna of 1814–15 by the 19th-century French painter Jean Baptiste Isabey. Emperor Napoleon I and Empress Josephine of France had once been the artist's patrons. But this picture depicted statesmen (though in life they never stood in the same room) who put a stop to Napoleon's conquests and negotiated to restore peace and stability throughout Europe. They laid the diplomatic groundwork for the movement called the Restoration. It had been the earlier First Treaty of Paris, signed on May 30, 1814, that designated the Austrian emperor to convene this congress in Vienna. In the aftermath of the French Revolution (1789–99) and of the Napoleonic Wars (1805–14), the Congress raised hopes that an enduring peace could be established in Europe.

Twenty-three of the Congress's leading diplomats appear together in Isabey's mythical portrayal. Once Napoleon's image filled the painter's canvasses. Now his brushes and pigments recorded the likenesses of those who would establish a new European order, without Napoleon. No actual heads of state are present, although Tsar Alexander I of Russia was a principal negotiator. The British foreign secretary, Viscount Robert Stewart Castlereagh, sits, slightly left of center, with his back toward the 76-year-old French diplomat Charles Maurice de Talleyrand-Périgord, survivor of the French Revolution and his

Though he struck sharply at political novelties and deviations, he was too close in spirit to Voltaire to be a tyrant; compared with an Adolf Hitler or a Joseph Stalin, Metternich was mild and humane.
—ARTHUR J. MAY
Metternich biographer

Emperor Francis II was the last Holy Roman Emperor. After Napoleon dissolved the Holy Roman Empire, he adopted the title of emperor of Austria (as Francis I).

The 1814–15 Congress of Vienna. Metternich (standing, sixth from left) guided the European nations toward a peaceful reconciliation after the defeat of Napoleon.

days as foreign minister under the despotic Napoleon. Seated in the foreground, and looking toward the others, is the Prussian prince Karl August von Hardenberg. Russian foreign minister Count Karl von Nesselrode stands at the shoulder of Pédro de Sousa Holstein, duke of Palmela, of Portugal. Standing behind Talleyrand is the Austrian Friedrich von Gentz, secretary of the Congress. He confers with Baron Wilhelm von Humboldt of Prussia. On the left, and farthest from the conference table, stands Arthur Wellesley, the first duke of Wellington, who looks intently at the leading figure of the Congress, the Austrian foreign minister Prince Klemens von Metternich. Metternich stands with his right hand uplifted, palm upward, as if weighing something in it or perhaps pointing toward Castlereagh.

It was Metternich who put himself forward as the Congress's most important mediator. He was the chief architect of a general European peace, intended to be satisfactory to all participants. He would strive to turn a military alliance into a lasting political order. Gentz remarked that it was fortunate that these various ministers never encountered one another at the same time. Instead, during the early-morning hours they met informally in Metternich's apartment on the Ballplatz in Vienna, the capital of Habsburg-ruled Austria. The reigning monarchs

Emperor Francis I of Austria, Tsar Alexander I of Russia, King Frederick William III of Prussia, and King Frederick Augustus I of Saxony regularly reviewed these discussions. The Great Powers, or the Big Four, consisting of Russia, Austria, Prussia, and Great Britain, subsequently became the Big Five when Talleyrand was admitted to the Congress to represent France in January 1815.

On March 6, in the city of Vienna, Metternich saw a conference finally concluded at 3:00 A.M. It had begun in his apartments the previous evening among representatives of the Great Powers. The representatives of the Big Five had finished discussing the fate of the German state of Saxony, ruled by King Frederick Augustus I. In 1809 the Saxons had fought alongside the armies of Napoleon. Over Frederick Augustus's protests, it was decided that he must cede three-fifths of his kingdom to Prussia. After he saw the Saxon dispute brought to a close, Metternich decided to retire to his chambers to sleep. He left instructions with his servants that he was not to be disturbed. He had slept for only three

This political cartoon satirizes Metternich's attempts to maintain a balance of power in Europe amid the ruling monarchs' push for territorial gains.

hours when a messenger arrived with an urgent dispatch from the imperial and royal consul-general of Genoa in Italy. The valet, seeing that the message was urgent, ignored Metternich's instructions, woke him, and presented him with the message. The foreign minister awoke briefly and took the message without reading it. At 7:30 A.M. he awoke with a start, tore open the dispatch, and read the following:

> The English commissioner Campbell has just entered the harbour enquiring whether any-one had seen Napoleon at Genoa, in view of the fact that he had disappeared from the island of Elba. The answer being in the negative, the English frigate put to sea without further delay.

An 1810 map of Europe demonstrates the extent of Napoleon's power prior to his abdication on April 11, 1814.

Within minutes Metternich informed Francis I of the alarming news. The shocked Austrian emperor stated, "Our business is to give the world repose

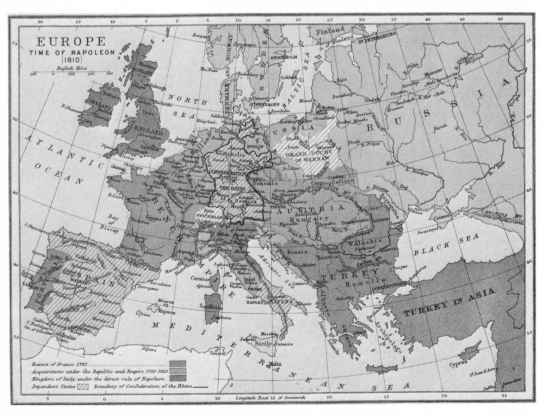

which he [Napoleon] has troubled all these years."
Next, the foreign minister went to the tsar of Russia
and to the king of Prussia. Both assured Metternich
that they would do all they could to prevent Napoleon once more from threatening the peace of Europe. "At 10 the Ministers of the Four Powers had
gathered . . . in my study," Metternich wrote.

No European diplomat understood the magnitude
of this emergency better than Metternich. The former emperor of France, who had humiliated Austrian armies four times between 1797 and 1809,
was again at large. After coming ashore in France,
Napoleon declared ominously, "The Congress is
dissolved."

The paths of Metternich and Napoleon had
crossed before in important and strange ways. Metternich received his first diplomatic appointment in
1801, when he was made envoy to Saxony for the
Habsburg rulers of Austria. (That same year, Castlereagh, who would become Metternich's British
counterpart at the Congress, was elected to the
Union House of Commons, an office he held until
1822.) When Metternich later served as Austrian
ambassador to France between 1806 and 1809, he
was in a unique position to see the pandemonium
that Napoleon's desire for conquest inflicted on Europe. Napoleon himself, as French emperor, had re-
quested that Metternich be appointed to this post.
While in Paris, Metternich saw the military genius
from Corsica rapidly scale the heights of power and
crown himself emperor of France. Beginning in
1809, Metternich, as foreign minister, labored for
five years to build an international coalition against
the fierce soldier, whose ambitions routinely chal-
lenged political borders and neighboring rulers.
Having broken France's hold on Austria, starting in
1812, Metternich maneuvered Austrian foreign policy into a direct collision with Napoleon. On August
10, 1813, Austria declared war on Napoleon. By the
spring of 1814, Metternich obtained the alliance
necessary to end Napoleon's ruthless campaign.

Prior to the Congress there had been another major conference. After the First Treaty of Paris, reign-

Napoleon I, declared em-
peror of France in 1804, became the king of Italy in
1805. One of the greatest
conquerors in world history,
Napoleon nearly succeeded
in dominating all of Europe.

After his abdication in 1814, Napoleon was exiled to the island of Elba. Before the Congress of Vienna had concluded, Napoleon escaped the island and marched into Paris, temporarily returning to his position as emperor of France.

ing monarchs of the allied nations had traveled to London. Alexander was the most outspoken and arrogant ruler at these meetings, hosted by Great Britain. Rather than establish positive ties with the British and the French, he offended them. Little was accomplished, and the tsar proved uncooperative about scheduling the Congress of Vienna. Alexander's already high opinion of himself reached astronomical heights after Napoleon's downfall and retreat in 1812, when the Russian winter destroyed his invading force against the tsar. By insisting on making unreasonable demands on nearly every major statesman, the tsar lost a chance to make further negotiations unnecessary. He was blatantly rude to George IV, the prince regent and the conference's host. Metternich attended this conference, but the reception he received was somewhat cool because the Austrian emperor did not make the trip to London.

After trying to fight Austrian and Prussian armies on French soil, Napoleon failed to halt the allies, who took Paris on March 31, 1814. In April, Alexander and Frederick William met with Napoleon's plenipotentiaries, Marshal Ney, duke of Elchingen, and Marshal MacDonald, duke of Taranto, to accept Napoleon's renunciation of the French throne. The Senate, which had been little more than his servant while he was emperor, proclaimed its former master deposed.

Sent into exile, Napoleon sailed to the island of Elba, off the Italian coast, where he would be its reigning monarch. That same month, Louis XVIII of the House of Bourbon, France's traditional ruling dynasty, landed in France. To his surprise, the Senate named him "King of France and Navarre."

Metternich was astounded when the French treated Napoleon so leniently by allowing him to reign over a miniature empire on the island of Elba. Now that Napoleon had returned to France with 1,500 troops, Metternich had to try to overcome the disunity within the Congress. Knowing of this disunity, Napoleon saw a clear opportunity to regain a foothold on the European continent. While quarreling over the spoils made available to them with Napoleon's collapse, the victors seemed to forget that it was Napoleon's insatiable ambition that had originally brought them together. The renewed threat posed by Napoleon served to revive their former unity.

Gloomy as the prospect of warfare was, Metternich recognized that their common foe would serve to put a stop to bickering among the allies. On March 13, Napoleon was declared an outlaw and a "disturber of world repose" by Austria, Great Britain, Prussia, Russia, Portugal, Sweden — and France. Against the renegade Napoleon, the Great Powers could raise nearly 800,000 soldiers.

On March 19, Louis took leave of Paris, traveling first to Lille, where he encountered resistance, and then proceeded to Ghent. Despite this apparent triumph, however, Napoleon sensed something was wrong; later he recalled that his confidence had been shaken. "I had an instinctive feeling that the outcome would prove unfortunate," he noted. A new grand alliance was under way. A member of the Austrian delegation to the Congress was put in charge of having the necessary agreements printed. The task fell to Gentz. Gentz had first met Metternich in 1801 when the latter was the Austrian representative in Dresden, Saxony. Twelve years later Gentz was Metternich's personal secretary. In 1814 he was recognized as the highly able secretary to the Con-

King Frederick Wilhelm II of Prussia was defeated by Napoleon in 1807. By signing the Treaty of Tilsit in July 1807, he surrendered the control of Prussia to the French.

Alexander I, tsar of Russia, also signed the Treaty of Tilsit, which left Napoleon the most powerful monarch on the continent. However, when French troops invaded Russia in 1912, Alexander created the Holy Alliance against Napoleon.

gress of Vienna. Gentz was entrusted, that fateful March, with making the results of the Congress public. The Congress, like almost all diplomatic sessions, was the business of aristocratic statesmen. Until this time it was customary for diplomacy to be conducted in secrecy. Treaties and agreements were made in secret and not made a part of the public record. Foreign ministers informally met at Metternich's apartments, usually in the early morning. Their activities were reviewed by the kings for whom they negotiated. Lesser powers and principalities were consulted only when the Big Four (or Council of Ministers) considered it necessary. This practice continued after the Big Four became the Big Five. Spying and deception were commonplace, with mistresses playing an important role in these activities. Of the four mistresses with whom Metternich became involved during the Congress, two had been associated with Alexander. Although each power was scrambling for its own territorial interests at the Congress, Metternich did envision a grand scheme: the balance of power. In 1806 Gentz, a talented publicist and journalist, wrote in his *Fragments on the Balance of Power in Europe* that the various nations that composed the "state system" would create "the general union of all European powers in one connecting system." The theory of balance of power was not new and certainly not radical. A British commentary dating from 1741 called it "an equal Distribution of Power among the Princes of Europe; one makes it impracticable for the one to disturb the Repose of the other." Two tasks were Metternich's to accomplish after Napoleon's defeat in 1814. He had to find a way to suppress a resurgence of Napoleon's power, and he had to prevent any other conquering force from overturning European peace and security.

Because it was impossible to balance the European state system without France, Metternich had resolved to obtain the cooperation of the French. His most important concern with regard to France was to contain the forces of war and political radicalism that the French Revolution had unleashed. In their work at the Congress, Metternich and Castlereagh most clearly recognized the need for statesmen who could rise above their own individual interests.

Alexander and Hardenberg, the Prussian foreign minister, were usually reluctant to compromise their territorial aims. They were headstrong about these issues. Frederick William wanted all of Saxony; Alexander wanted to create a new Poland under his own direction. According to historian Harold Nicolson, Alexander's designs on Poland were a murky business that "was constantly confusing and sapping the unity of the coalition."

However, Napoleon had returned to France, regained the allegiance of his former general Marshal Ney, and proceeded, as Metternich predicted he would, to Paris. Talleyrand soon closed ranks with Metternich and Castlereagh. It had been Talleyrand who had masterminded the Bourbon king's return to the French throne. This action stemmed from Talleyrand's firm defense of legitimacy, meaning that power rightfully belonged to a country's traditional rulers, not to foreign usurpers. Legitimacy was one pillar of balance-of-power diplomacy. The second pillar was equilibrium, which meant that nations, although of unequal strength, should not

It is not a momentary equilibrium which ought to be established, but a durable equilibrium.
—M. DE TALLEYRAND
Foreign minister under Napoleon, on the balance of power

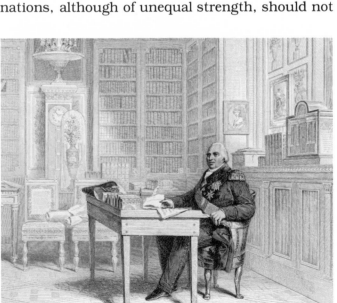

Louis XVIII was restored to the French throne after the 1814 downfall of Napoleon. Upon Napoleon's return from Elba, Louis fled from Paris but was again crowned king of France after Napoleon's defeat at Waterloo in June, 1815.

Friedrich von Gentz was Metternich's personal secretary as well as the Austrian secretary at the Congress of Vienna. He was given the task of making public the agreements of the Congress.

Karl August Furst Hardenberg was the Prussian minister of foreign affairs (1804—06) and chancellor (1810—22). He bargained for Saxony during the Congress of Vienna and refused to compromise Prussia's territorial aims.

seek to overpower the legitimate government of another. Indeed, Metternich believed that individual states must submit to the larger state system — the so-called Metternich System. As the French representative to the Congress, Talleyrand knew it was important to cultivate good relations with Great Britain, the nation that had consistently resisted Napoleon. Talleyrand was an "equilibrist," but Castlereagh complained about the Frenchman's views on Russia and Poland. Castlereagh did not think the duke took a firm enough stance against Alexander and the threat of Russian expansion. Even Metternich worried that Alexander might become another Napoleon.

Alexander's stubborn defense of his own interests was tested against his loyalty to the Coalition opposed to Napoleon. Napoleon, on his return to power, discovered a secret treaty between Metternich, Castlereagh, and Talleyrand against the Prussians and Russians. After Louis fled to Paris, Napoleon sent a copy of this agreement, made in January 1815, to the tsar. Alexander assured Metternich that he was not offended by this past agreement. Having been promised most of Saxony only two days after reports of Napoleon's disappearance from Genoa, Prussia was also ready to stand with the allies.

Napoleon was still accustomed to getting his way by resorting to brute force. The Napoleon of 1815, however, was no longer the same in the eyes of his opponents. Nineteenth-century Scottish essayist and historian Thomas Carlyle writes, "The world was not disposed to be down-trodden underfoot; to be bound into masses and built together, as he liked, for a pedestal to France and him; the world had quite other purposes in view."

Metternich rose to fame in a prolonged contest with Napoleon and prevailed. He went on to create a stable international arrangement on the European continent that would last for more than 30 years. He wrote to Alexander in 1820, "The labours to which [the masses] must devote themselves are too continuous and too positive to allow them to

throw themselves into the uncertainties of abstract ambitions."

He was appointed chancellor of the Austrian empire in 1821. From then onward, he refused to give in to three ideas that were increasingly popular on the continent: liberalism, with its emphasis on liberty; democracy, emphasizing equality; and nationalism, a desire for unity and independence among national groups. Metternich once explained to Prince Paul Esterhazy of Austria that "the calculated liberals" resembled "opportunists who break into houses which they set on fire, not to save the valuables, but to make off with them." To him the "so-called *perfecting of society* [the representative system]" produced only "piles of rubble."

Metternich clearly understood that democracy rested upon the principles of liberty, or freedom, and equality. But he had nothing but contempt for both: "Two words suffice to create evil; two words which because they are devoid of any practical meaning delight the visionaries. The words are *liberty*, and *equality*." Democracy was alien to his autocratic view of society and the state. To him Europe faced a simple choice between revolution and restoration. The practical question became how to steer ships of state through a storm of chaos and set a course on which there were no storms and no chance of mutiny.

Metternich opened the Congress of Vienna with a series of parties at his home. The parties were followed by sessions of hard bargaining among the Big Five nations (Austria, Russia, Prussia, Britain, and France).

2

Rustlings of Discontent

There was little in Metternich's early life that fore-shadowed his unusual achievements later on. His childhood was typical for a child raised a member of a noble household, based for many years in the Rhineland. This area was home to the rural gentry and was influenced by both French-speaking and German-speaking cultures because of its location on the French border. Klemens Wenzel Nepomuk Lothar von Metternich-Winneburg-Beilstein was born on May 15, 1773, in the Rhenish town of Koblenz. The family estates at Winneburg and Beilstein were located nearby. Another estate belonged to the Metternichs at Königswart, Bohemia, some 300 miles nearer to Vienna, the center of Habsburg rule.

Metternich's father, Franz Georg, was a Rhenish *Reichsgraf*, an imperial count, with representation in the parliament, or *Reichstag*, at Regensburg and the parliamentary Council of Counts in the German state of Westphalia. The family was based at the Moselle River between Trier and Koblenz, with Winneburg on the left bank of the river and Beilstein on the right. Property in the Rhineland produced enough income for the Metternich family to live comfortably in Koblenz and remain somewhat above the lower nobility.

His mother, the Countess Beatrice von Kagenegg,

Anton Graff's crayon sketch of Metternich (1803) portrays the 30-year-old Austrian statesman at the beginning of his long diplomatic career.

A leading figure in the French Enlightenment, the Swiss-French political theorist and philosopher Jean-Jacques Rousseau argued that man is inherently good in his natural state but is corrupted by society.

Metternich was strongly influenced by the work of Charles de Secondat, Baron Montesquieu. A follower of John Locke, Montesquieu advocated the separation and balance of power within the governmental structure.

took a lively interest in the education of her children, including Klemens's older sister, Pauline, and his younger brother, Joseph. Although her family came from the German city of Breisgai, she preferred the culture of France and spoke French with her children. French became Metternich's favorite language. His fluency in French would prove important to his future career. All of the youngsters received instruction in the Catholic faith from a cleric, the Abbé Bertrand. Their tutor, Johann Friedrich Simon, gave them a less conventional, more experimental, education. Thus the children were raised as Roman Catholics and at the same time were exposed to the doctrines and discoveries of the Enlightenment, a secular movement that influenced the arts and sciences.

Simon was typical of those who taught the values of the Enlightenment. His background was middle class and Protestant. Although religious background varied, the Enlightenment won over many middle-class professionals, who were increasingly interested in political freedom. They also were fascinated by the discovery of physical laws in the universe and by scientific invention.

Simon did not neglect his young student's physical training. He had taught for two years in the experimental school in Dessau, run by the German educator Johann Bernhard Basedon. Basedon believed in the classical notion of sound body and sound mind. Under Simon's tutelage, Metternich became a superb swimmer and retained a swimmer's build for most of his life. The Philanthropinum, as Basedon's school was called, utilized the psychological theories of 18th-century philosopher John Locke and the progressive educational doctrine developed by the French political philosopher Jean-Jacques Rousseau, the widely celebrated author of *Social Contract*, which discussed mankind's enslavement by unjust governments. Rousseau also argued that civilizations had enchained human beings, whose natural state was freedom. Obedience, he asserted, "is only due to legitimate powers." Rousseau believed children should be educated first through their senses rather than through the intellect alone, whereas Locke argued that all knowledge and ideas derive from experience. A leading political theorist at this time, he wrote *Two Treatises on Government*, in which he emphasized the need for governments to be founded upon the principle of liberty. Metternich's tutor was also enthusiastic about the writings of François Marie Arouet de Voltaire. Voltaire, a scathing satirist, was one of the central figures in the French intellectual movement led by the Encyclopedists, the compilers of the *Encyclopedé* (*Encyclopedia*).

In November 1788, after tutoring the count and countess's children for four years, Simon took Klemens and his younger brother Joseph to the University of Strasbourg. Countess Metternich later wrote to her oldest son, "In Germany you must admire German music and in France French music; it is like that with most things" — practical advice for adapting to a new social environment. It was also advice befitting a future diplomat. There the two boys were introduced to Prince Maximilian from the House of Wittlesbach, and he became their guardian. In 1805, Prince Max would become the first king of Bavaria. At present he commanded the Royal Regiment of Alsace. His wife was a good friend of the children's mother. Klemens and Joseph were thus placed in protective hands, and Simon remained with them in Strasbourg.

For Metternich, Strasbourg was another world compared with Koblenz. In the summer of 1786, the family had visited the estate in Bohemia, Metternich's first exposure to the broader Habsburg domain. Here were students from beyond Germany and France; there were Swiss, English, and Russians, aristocrats and commoners. Of his professors, Metternich best remembered Christopher Wilhelm Koch, who lectured on law and on the history of revolutions. Koch was a follower of another French thinker of the Enlightenment, Charles de Secondat, Baron Montesquieu, whose book *The Spirit of the Laws* made him one of 18th-century France's most astute social philosophers. He, like Locke, saw a need for several branches within government, each being a check on the other. Montes-

John Locke (1632–1704) founded the school of philosophy called British empiricism, which rejected the existence of innate ideas, arguing instead that all knowledge is acquired through experience.

Lower-class involvement in the French Revolution began with the storming of the Paris prison-fortress called the Bastille on July 14, 1789. Bastille Day is today a national holiday in France.

quieu's ideas were taken up and circulated widely by the Encyclopedists, led by Denis Diderot. Through Koch, Metternich first became acquainted with these and other concepts of the period. The concept of political checks and balances much appealed to the young Metternich.

It was in Strasbourg that Metternich had his first experience with revolutionary violence. It was set off by the fall of the Bastille, a prison-fortress in Paris, on July 14, 1789, as the French Revolution, which began with the National Assembly's defiance toward King Louis XVI, became violent. By July 20 the news had reached the population of Strasbourg, who became agitated at once. On Tuesday, a mob stormed the city hall, or *Stadthaus*. Metternich later recorded in his memoirs: "Surrounded by a number of dull spectators who called themselves the people, I had been present at the plundering of the *Stadthaus*, perpetrated by a drunken mob, which considered itself the people."

So traumatic was the effect of this event that in his later years he still recalled the revolution with particular bitterness. "A configuration, which grew with each day, laid waste the neighboring kingdom. Thoughtful men already saw the influence which this must, sooner or later, exercise beyond the boundaries of France." He noted that as a student he did not anticipate the powerful impact the French Revolution would have on all Europe: "I saw only . . . contrast between the country contaminated by Jacobinism [the outlook of the revolutionary Jacobins, who, for a time, controlled the revolution] and the country where human grandeur was united with a noble national spirit."

The events of Strasbourg in 1789 were not really so dramatic. That summer a mob did, in fact, storm the city hall and break into the wine cellar, but order was quickly restored by the local regiment of Royal Guards under the command of Metternich's guardian, Prince Maximilian. Two days later, a single looter was hanged for allegedly stealing coins from the city hall. Quiet again stole over the university town. Metternich continued his studies for another year.

Although Metternich was shocked at this revolutionary fervor, his former tutor began publishing a revolutionary journal in Strasbourg. Simon translated the Declaration of the Rights of Man and Citizen, the basic statement of French revolutionary principles, into German. Simon traveled to Paris to join the ranks of the Jacobins, or members of the Jacobin Club. The Jacobins were devoted to democratic principles and opposed to monarchy. But for these causes they put thousands to their deaths on the guillotine under their principal leader, Maximilien Robespierre. Metternich reported that his tutor "made himself notorious in Paris," particularly in August and September 1792. Simon was still in Paris when Metternich was appointed ambassador to France 14 years later. Metternich discovered him teaching the German language at the College de Louis le Grand, where Robespierre and other French revolutionaries had been educated. When Napoleon became first consul of France at age 30, after defeating the Second Coalition, which opposed revolutionary France, he decided to eliminate the Jacobins. Many were imprisoned, and Simon lost his teaching position. Metternich once noted that Simon had "never attempted to influence my opin-

> *I suffer no illusions and I always see the strings that work the puppets while the foolish public exhausts itself looking for mechanical processes.*
> —PRINCE METTERNICH
> on his political insight

ions." By this he meant that Simon never attempted to indoctrinate him in Jacobinism. However, when the Bourbons, whom the Jacobins had violently overthrown, returned to Paris, the duke of Orleans made Simon a tutor to his children.

As young men, the lives of Metternich and Napoleon (only four years older than Metternich) began to connect — if only indirectly. As Metternich described in his memoirs: "The year I went there [Strasbourg], the youthful Napoleon Bonaparte had just left; he concluded his studies in the artillery regiment quartered at Strasbourg. We had the same professors for mathematics and fencing — a circumstance which was only remembered by those masters when the little artillery officer became, step by step, a great General, First Consul, and afterward emperor. During my residence in Strasbourg I never heard his name mentioned." Then, in a footnote: "In passing through Strasbourg in 1808, I had a visit from my old fencing master, Mons. Fustet. 'Is it not a strange thing,' said he to me, 'that it was my lot to give you fencing lessons, just after I had given the like to Napoleon? I hope that my two pupils, the Emperor of the French and the Austrian Ambassador to Paris, will not take into their heads to come to blows with each other.' "

At the age of 17, Metternich transferred from the University of Strasbourg to that of Mainz. The skyline of Mainz, located on the Rhine, is dominated by the towers of its 10th-century Romanesque cathedral.

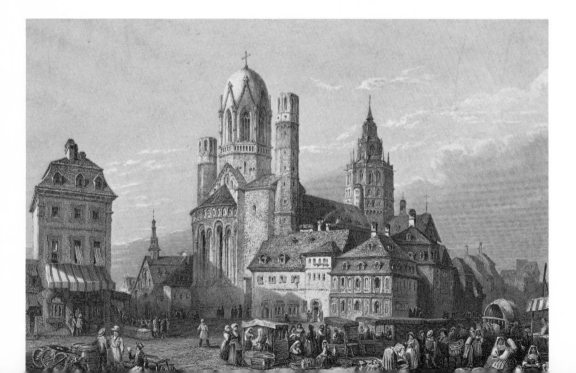

In 1790, Metternich transferred to the University of Mainz to study law. In Mainz, he also attended lectures on the history of the Germanic states given by Professor Nicholas Vogt. They reinforced the views of Koch at Strasbourg, who had emphasized that territorial princes were important to maintaining the balance of power in the German Empire (*Reich*), Vogt stressed the significance of all the states, including the ecclesiastical states, belonging to the Holy Roman Empire of the German Nations. According to him, they maintained another form of checks and balances within the empire. Both professors called this arrangement "the just equilibrium." Concepts of equilibrium between states formed the bedrock of Metternich's political doctrine. His beliefs were so similar to Vogt's that they became lasting friends. There were other lecturers, but Metternich took what he needed from his studies and applied the lessons as he went. He believed that proper opinions were based upon experience and practical results.

During the time when Metternich was studying at Strasbourg and Mainz, his father had been appointed minister of the Imperial Court to the elector of Trier. (Electors were rulers of states that were part of the Holy Roman Empire. Under the Holy Roman system electors were empowered to elect the

Because of the dangers of the war between Austria and France, Metternich and his family fled the Hague and settled in Vienna, where in later years Metternich would serve as Austria's foreign minister.

King Louis XVI of France plunged his country into bankruptcy. In October 1789 mobs stormed the royal palace at Versailles and forced the evacuation of the royal family. Under the 1791 Constitution Louis was guillotined in January 1793.

Holy Roman emperor.) Franz Georg's duties to the House of Habsburg later extended to the archbishops of Cologne and Mainz, the other two ecclesiastical electors in the Rhineland and finally all of the state of Westphalia. In October 1790, Metternich left Strasbourg because his father summoned him to attend the coronation of the Holy Roman Emperor Leopold II at Frankfurt, where Franz Georg had just been promoted to Austrian ambassador. Two years later Leopold died, not long after forming an alliance with Prussia against France in the War of the First Coalition. Acting as representative for both the Rhenish ecclesiastical electorates and the Bohemian aristocracy at the coronation, it was Metternich's father's chance to gain prominence in Austria's ruling circles. The family arrived in Frankfurt with a spectacular retinue. Ninety-eight coaches carried them grandly into the city. Despite royal disapproval of this ostentatiousness, young Metternich met Archduke Francis, who would become the last Holy Roman emperor as Francis II in 1792 until abdicating in 1806 but would remain emperor of Austria until 1835 as Francis I.

In December 1790, Franz Georg was appointed minister plenipotentiary to the States General of the Austrian Netherlands (now Belgium) in Brussels. The elder Metternich was not well suited to this position. But his son now had the opportunity to work in Brussels in the foreign office there. Metternich became familiar with the court of the elector and began one of many liaisons that were to characterize his social — and diplomatic — life. He became romantically involved with Marie-Constance de Caumont la Force, daughter of Comte de Lamoignon, the departed keeper of the seals for the French king, Louis XVI, who was executed by the revolutionary National Convention in 1793. That this young woman was married did not deter Metternich. However, he did not ignore any of the social advantages the affair might have occasioned. Able to polish his already considerable social abilities and charm, he later recalled, "My residence in Mainz was of the greatest use to me and had a decided influence on my life. My time was divided between my studies and . . . a society as distinguished for intellectual superiority as for the social position of its members." At age 17, Metternich probably did not acknowledge his own conservative viewpoint, but he enjoyed the privileges and high expectations that were his as an aristocrat.

In March 1792, Emperor Leopold died and was succeeded by his son, the archduke Francis. Again, at the coronation of Francis, Metternich played a part in the ceremony. Klemens was put in charge of the banquet and opened the ball with Princess Louise of Mecklenburg, who later became a favorite queen in Prussia. Yet elegant balls and ceremonies could not hide the tension that accompanied Francis's accession to the throne. When war was declared on Austria in March 1792, the wars of the French Revolution began. Metternich went to Brussels and joined his father. His formal education was at an end as Austria began fighting not merely against an aggressive neighbor but one that wanted to export its revolution to other nations.

In September an Austrian army, which had been assembled at Koblenz under the command of the duke of Brunswick, was defeated by the French at Valmy. By October the French pressed on to Mainz and seized Frankfurt. The French general François Dumouriez advanced toward Brussels. Austrians were forced to flee the city. Karl Wilhelm Ferdinand, duke of Brunswick (who later invaded France), maintained his headquarters in Koblenz, but the Metternich family fled the town. Their estates at Winneburg and Beilstein were devastated as the conflict raged. After the tide of battle turned against the French in the spring of 1793, Metternich and

The French general Charles-François Dumouriez won several important battles after his country declared war on Austria in April 1792. Defeated in 1793, Dumouriez eventually deserted the French army to join the Austrian forces.

his family returned to Brussels. The previous year the revolutionaries in France had declared their country a republic and in January 1793 had done away with the embodiment of monarchy there by imposing a death sentence on the king.

In Brussels, Metternich met Frederick, duke of York, son of King George III, who had led an expeditionary force of British and German troops from Hesse and Hanover in the recent military campaign. This acquaintance with the duke of York proved helpful to the younger Metternich when his father arranged to send him to Great Britain on a special financial mission from the Netherlands. He was warmly received and well treated throughout his stay in London, during which time he received the title of ambassador extraordinary and minister plenipotentiary of the Hague, the Dutch capital. On this visit he met important and influential people, such as William Pitt (who later did much to shape British foreign policy), Charles Fox, the prince of

This caricature portrays Napoleon and William Pitt, prime minister of England, claiming portions of the globe for themselves. Metternich met Pitt on his visit to London in 1793.

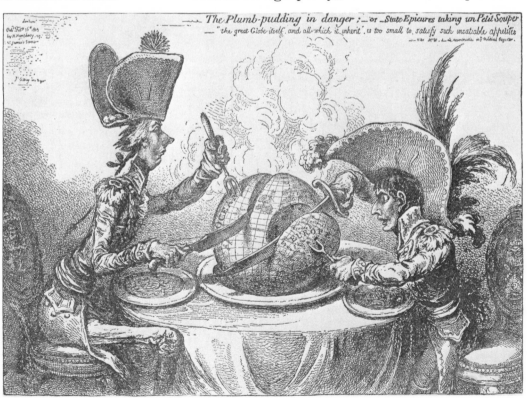

The Plumb-pudding in danger ; or _State Epicures taking un Petit Souper_
— "the great Globe itself, and all which it inherit", is too small to satisfy such insatiable appetites

Wales, and King George IV. Significantly, he also met the Irish member of Parliament Edmund Burke, who in 1790 had taken a strong stand against the French Revolution with a formidable book, *Reflections on the Revolution in France*. Metternich managed to elude disaster and make it back to the Hague.

Burke rejected popular sovereignty, the principle that the citizens of a nation should be able to govern themselves. He also upheld monarchy and denounced natural rights (the principle that nature endowed humanity with certain self-evident rights). Burke attacked the French Declaration of the Rights of Man and Citizen, which echoed ideas set forth in the American Declaration of Independence. To Burke historical precedent, custom, and tradition were the practical foundation for law and government. Metternich admired what he saw of Great Britain's government, and Burke's defense of the established order. Burke also wrote on "the similitude throughout Europe of religion, laws and manners." Metternich's subsequent defense of a state system was reinforced by Burke's thinking. Metternich would share the conservative thinker's view that the power of France should be contained. When Simon, Metternich's former tutor, had translated and published the Declaration of the Rights of Man and Citizen, Metternich's future associate, Gentz, had begun translating Burke's most famous work into German. Thus political theories that would dominate the Congress of Vienna more than 20 years later were already being forged and spread throughout Europe.

Meanwhile, the conflict with France delayed Metternich's return to the Netherlands in the summer of 1794. Danger was not far away during this adventure. Metternich managed to reach the Hague even though his ship was blown off course — right into a naval battle. Once more the family had to beat a hasty retreat to the temporary seat of the Dutch government on the lower Rhine. From there, they decided to go to Vienna. Within 15 years, Metternich would reside there as foreign minister of the entire Austrian Empire.

Edmund Burke, political writer and Irish member of the British Parliament, opposed the French Revolution, believing the people of the nation incapable of governing themselves without established law and order.

3

Ambassador's Apprenticeship

In late autumn of 1794 Metternich saw the imperial capital of Austria for the first time. As Rhinelanders, the Metternichs were, for the most part, outsiders in that city. Their estates on the Moselle had been lost. In addition, the emperor was displeased with the elder Metternich, who, as ambassador to the Netherlands, had tried to organize a militia of peasants from noble estates in the Austrian Netherlands to combat the French. When the effort failed and the Netherlands went over to the French the following year, the emperor blamed the result on arming the peasants. Metternich's father was blamed for not consulting Vienna, and the emperor abolished his post. In Bohemia (now Czechoslovakia) the family still owned an estate, which had been long neglected since Metternich's childhood. It was now a last remaining resource to which his family could turn. Klemens spent November and December overseeing the family estate at Königswart. His parents went to Vienna to arrange a marriage for their oldest son.

They found an eligible young woman with a more than adequate social background. Largely at the instigation of Metternich's mother, Countess Kagenegg, contacts were made with the Kaunitz family, one of the most prestigious in Viennese society. In

The Austrian prince built a legendary reputation for diplomatic finesse and devotion to public duty. It was not a case, however, of all work and no play, for he delighted in parties and he was fond of ladies.
—ARTHUR J. MAY
Metternich biographer

During the coup of 18 Brumaire on November 9, 1799, Napoleon overthrew the French Directory, the executive branch of the government, and set up the Consulate with himself as dictator.

Napoleon addresses the Rhine League, a confederation that would form the nucleus of a Pan-European Confederation.

her youth, Metternich's mother had been the childhood friend of the Princess von Oettingen-Spielburg, who later married Ernst von Kaunitz. They had an only child, a 19-year-old daughter, Eleonore. Certainly, it seemed to Countess Kagenegg that her son Klemens was the perfect suitor for Eleonore von Kaunitz. Metternich's mother had vivid childhood memories of the court under Maria Theresa, empress of Austria from 1740 to 1780. She remembered Eleonore's grandfather, who was the statesman Prince Wenzel Anton von Kaunitz. He was influential in bringing about the Diplomatic Revolution, which took place between the War of the Austrian Succession (1740—48) and the Seven Years' War (1756—63). Kaunitz considered Prussia rather than France the main threat to Austria. Centuries of Habsburg foreign policy were reversed, as a result, when Austria abandoned Prussia as an ally and became allied to France. Great Britain became Prussia's ally.

On her father's estate at Austerlitz on September 27, 1795, Eleonore von Kaunitz married Metternich. Thus another kind of alliance was established. Metternich gained admission to the uppermost social and political ranks in Vienna. His career as a courtier was about to begin.   Although the couple had been brought together by their parents, Klemens and Eleonore managed to be compatible and to acquire considerable property. Secure in his now even higher social status and cultivated in the manners of the nobility, Metternich already had accumulated substantial firsthand knowledge of political matters and several influential contacts. Handsome and debonair, he possessed talent and poise.

For two years, there was little more to do other than dabble in science and enjoy his elevated status. He and Eleonore began a family when a daughter, Marie, was born in January 1797. Not all obstacles to political advancement had been magically removed. Eleonore's father was not entirely convinced that the personable young Metternich was the right man for his only daughter. He stipulated that the couple would continue to live with him and that Metternich would not take a diplomatic post until after his death. But Kaunitz died suddenly in September.

Metternich, meanwhile, had not seemed anxious about a political career. A new ruling body known as the Directory had come to power in France. While serving the Directory in what became the Italian campaigns, Napoleon quickly proved his magnificent talent for military strategy by winning battle after battle. He forced the surrender of Italian states and he battered the Austrians. On October 17, Napoleon concluded the Treaty of Campo-Formio with Austria. Strangely, his homeland's defeat was a stroke of luck for Metternich, who would soon begin an ascent to the dizzying heights of international politics.

In the Treaty of Campo-Formio, Napoleon forced the Austrians to recognize both the French annexation of territory later to become the kingdom of Belgium and the Rhineland as the eastern boundary of France. Under the treaty, northern Italy became a French dependency. Napoleon's treaty terms also provided that compensation was to be made to the Austrians for the loss to France of the entire left bank of the Rhine River. A congress would be con-

> *I have two ears but only one mouth. I can listen to both sides of any question, but I can only say the same thing to different parties.*
> —PRINCE METTERNICH

vened for that purpose. The Austrians wanted to stall for time. They hoped to strengthen their bargaining position in the meantime. The Austrian foreign office was in the midst of negotiations with Great Britain and Prussia. Bavaria and the Rhineland were important territorial concerns to the Habsburg monarchy. Franz Georg Von Metternich was selected to negotiate a delay of the final settlement. Because he was a noble from the Rhineland, he was considered best able to understand the problems facing the Rhenish princes.

The congress began in Rastatt in December 1797. The count served as the Holy Roman Empire's representative. As at the previous imperial coronations, he was accompanied by his 24-year-old son, who again represented the counts of Westphalia. Neither father nor son received the confidence of the other Austrian delegates, who found them no more trustworthy than the French. Unfortunately, there was virtually no chance of a settlement being reached. The fate of the Rhineland had been sealed in 1795 at Basel, when Prussia withdrew from the

In this painting by Guillon, Napoleon negotiates the Treaty of Campo-Formio in October 1797 with representatives of the defeated Austria.

antirevolutionary coalition after being defeated by France.

Napoleon himself never made an expected appearance at Rastatt. The congress became a series of social events, and the actual diplomacy was carried on by the inner court circles. Despite doubts among fellow Austrian delegates about whether the Metternichs knew the terms of the Treaty of Campo-Formio, the younger Metternich saw that family interests were at stake. The French, whom Metternich described as being "more savage than white bears," instructed the Austrians to give up the left bank in return for compensation in Bavaria. Metternich wrote to his wife: "Everything is gone to the devil and the time is come when everyone must save from the wreck what he can." Thus Metternich undertook to protect his own interests, which were still those of a Rhinelander.

Metternich was caught between the larger interests of the Habsburgs and the interests of the provincial German princes. Although he did a good job of protecting family interests in the Rhineland, his presence at the Congress of Rastatt was visible but quiet. He remained in Rastatt until the middle of March 1799, when he returned to Vienna with his wife and daughter. His mission seemed to end peaceably when catastrophe struck.

The catastrophe was the Austrian declaration of war on France in 1798. This became the War of the Second Coalition, in which Austria counted Russia, Great Britain, and Turkey as allies. At this point, Austria was not strong enough, diplomatically or militarily, to take to the battlefield. The Habsburgs' difficulties were compounded by the *coup d'état* of 18th *Brumaire* (a month in the French Revolutionary calendar corresponding to November), which brought Napoleon to political power by abolishing the Directory and establishing the Consulate in France. By December, Napoleon was first consul and, effectively, dictator of France. Any Austrian defeat would now be handled directly by Napoleon. After a bold beginning for the Austrians, defeat was not far off. The Russians, then led by Tsar Paul,

The Prussian general Karl von Clausewitz fought in the wars against Napoleon. He later wrote *On War*, which describes the necessity for "total war."

Napoleon, on horseback, during the Battle of Marengo, in which the French armies triumphed over the Austrians. Napoleon's victory there was followed by the Treaty of Luneville.

soon grew disillusioned with their Austrian allies and withdrew support by 1800.

After Rastatt Metternich returned to Vienna, where Eleonore bore two more children. Another two years passed before he resumed his active political career. His major promotion was still 10 years away, his future hinging on the course of larger events — events that appeared to obey Napoleon's seemingly unconquerable will. In May 1800 Napoleon's armies crossed the Alps through the Great Saint Bernard pass and, in June, met the Austrians at Marengo. French reinforcements arrived just as the Austrians appeared to be winning, and Napoleon snatched victory from the jaws of defeat. The Austrians were crushed. Their fall at Marengo and at the Battle of Hohenlinden resulted in the Treaty of Lunéville, which solidified the terms of the unfavorable Treaty of Campo-Formio. It was signed on February 9, 1801. With the Rhineland now a dead issue, the days of the Holy Roman Empire were numbered. Napoleon had shifted the direction of the war from western Germany and the Rhineland to Northern Italy. There he could dictate the terms in both regions at the Habsburgs' expense.

Amid these bleak circumstances some light began

to shine on the path that lay before Metternich. He was presented with a choice of either serving the Imperial Diet at Regensburg or taking a new post in either Denmark or Saxony. Copenhagen, the capital of Denmark, did not seem sufficiently promising to further his career, and Regensburg had lost its attraction now that the Holy Roman Empire had become an all but meaningless concept after the Treaty of Lunéville. In February 1801, Metternich chose to serve as the emperor's representative at the Saxon court in the city of Dresden.

Metternich was now wholly in the service of the Habsburgs. His view of the dangers of revolution was unchanged, but he believed that Napoleon had tempered the revolutionary fever. Perhaps constructive diplomacy was still possible, he thought. It was his first responsible diplomatic assignment under the Habsburg emperor. For Metternich it was a unique vantage point from which to observe whether his conclusion was correct. He was not yet 30 years old.

During the next four years Metternich advanced rapidly in the service of Austria. Dresden, however, did not fulfill his expectations. He took time to write some "Instructions," but there was as yet little op-

In November 1803, Metternich accepted the position of Austrian ambassador to Prussia in Berlin. His social connection with Queen Louise's court proved helpful in his attempt to create an alliance among Austria, Prussia, and Russia.

portunity to put them into practice. Metternich was struck by the impact of only the previous 11 years on political circumstances. Already he was able to list several obstacles to building a stable European state system: "the fickle character of the Russian Emperor," "the existence of Poland," "the influence of Prussia in the affairs of the Empire," "the restoration of the European balance of power," and that "the neighborhood of Electoral Saxony will frequently necessitate negotiations which concern the welfare of our lands and the affairs of our subjects." Every item mentioned in the "Instructions" became a serious problem for the Congress of Vienna, 13 years later.

For the present, the court at Dresden was barely in touch with recent political events, and Metternich found it somewhat humdrum. He found some relief after meeting Gentz, who was creating a stir in central Europe with his translation of Burke's antirevolutionary writings. In addition to his friendship with Gentz, Metternich was cheered when he found himself a little nearer to gaining a similar assignment in Berlin, the Prussian capital.

During this period Metternich's lifelong penchant for romantic affairs came to light. Metternich already had developed a reputation for exploiting his good looks and charm while at Koblenz. This time, however, his liaison with Katharina Bagration, the former Countess Skavocouski of Latvia (now part of the Soviet Union), led to the birth of a daughter, Clementine, in 1802. Both Metternich and his wife recognized that he was the child's father, but it did not disrupt their marriage. That Metternich's marriage survived met with some amazement in Dresden. In January 1803, Eleonore gave birth to Viktor, Metternich's third son. Metternich went on to accumulate a series of mistresses who were a source of information and influence. He continued to use his successes with the opposite sex as an extension of diplomacy. Napoleon later called Metternich a "liar and an intriguer." The Austrians liking for intrigue did not place him above juggling extramarital relationships.

His appointment in January 1803 to serve as Austrian ambassador to Prussia in Berlin was a big step forward, and it indicated that Metternich was gradually gaining support among the ruling elite. Metternich did not actually arrive in Berlin until December, almost a year after his appointment. Berlin had a reputation for Spartan simplicity, a stamp put upon it both by the brilliant Prussian king Frederick the Great in the 18th century and by Prussia's rise as a key military power during the War of the Austrian Succession and the Seven Years' War. Metternich found Berlin rather dull, though not as stifling as Dresden.

One difference was the presence of Queen Louise, the princess with whom he had danced at the emperor Francis's coronation ball. He was "received as an old friend" upon his arrival and had innumerable opportunities to observe the members of the court at close range. This was important because the policymakers in Prussia were not much in agreement with one another. Metternich's primary task in Berlin, as he understood it, was to cultivate possibilities for an alliance between Austria, Prussia, and Russia. Such a policy objective had not been firmly set in Vienna. Still, it was a viable option, and one that was strategically worthwhile. This alliance was realized in 1805.

Metternich wanted to pursue his own policy within the framework of Habsburg interests. So he spent as much time as he could with the leading advisers at the court of Frederick William III. Among the king's advisers were members of the so-called war party in Prussia, such as Prince Karl August von Hardenberg, who became Prussian chancellor in 1810 and Freiherr Carl vom und zum Stein, who advanced administrative reform in Prussia and would later be instrumental in securing a Russo-Prussian alliance in 1813 (the Treaty of Kalisch, signed in February) while in exile in Russia under pressure from Napoleon. Finally, there was General Gerhard von Scharnhorst, who transformed the Prussian mercenary army into the people's army that would join the anti-French coalition of 1813. All three Prussians contributed decisively to Metternich's proposal to create this coalition, known as

General Gerhard von Scharnhorst, an adviser to King Frederick Wilhelm III of Prussia, assisted Metternich in his efforts to create a coalition between Russia, Prussia, and Austria.

Pope Pius VII traveled to Paris in 1804 to consecrate Napoleon as emperor. Four years later, however, Napoleon invaded Rome, an action for which Pius excommunicated him.

the Last Coalition. While not busy with diplomacy, he became involved with the princess Wilhelmina de Rohan, who, in Metternich's absence, spent time with Prince Louis Ferdinand.

Two things happened during these years that added weight to Metternich's position, though the consequences were not immediately apparent to everyone. They were also part of a larger pattern that had been revealed earlier at the Recess of Regensburg of 1803. In one way, the Recess of 1803 had merely compensated the Rhenish princes for their lost properties by transferring to them ecclesiastical land holdings — property of the Roman Catholic church. Thus relations between the church and the Habsburg monarchy were weakened. Secondly, regarding his family's personal interests, Metternich's negotiations at Rastatt allowed Franz Georg to obtain a new estate near Ulm, at Ochsenhausen, in Bavaria. The elder Metternich was also awarded the title of prince with a seat in the Imperial Diet.

The larger picture was hardly optimistic, however, for the power of France had displaced Austrian supremacy in Bavaria, Württemberg, and Baden. Napoleon claimed sovereignty in these areas and then moved to become hereditary emperor of France. This was approved by a plebiscite in May 1804 and was consecrated in Paris by Pope Pius VII at the Cathedral of Notre Dame on December 2, 1804.

Two years afterward, the crumbling Holy Roman Empire itself was officially abolished. As early as the beginning of 1805, this eventuality was clear to Metternich. In the interim, Napoleon's successful defense against the British at sea culminated in the Treaty of Amiens on March 27, 1802. By May 1803, Great Britain and Napoleon resumed the naval conflict that resulted in a brutal deadlock. Napoleon could not escape defeat indefinitely while dueling with the world's leading seagoing power. But prior to taking a pounding at the celebrated Battle of Trafalgar, Napoleon postponed invading Great Britain and sent the *Grande Armée* (Grand Army) to Bavaria. Surveying the emerging international situation while in Berlin, he realized that the old threat of the revolutionary Jacobins had only given way to the gigantic ambitions of Napoleon. Although the conditions were frustrating for this conservative to consider, the prospects for a stable system did not vanish from his mind. As historian Edward Vose Gulick puts it, "He [Metternich] was nothing if not flexible, and he never rested content with but one iron in the fire." Action had to be taken to forge a strong coalition against this new menace. To this end, Metternich lent all his efforts. As the Russians were negotiating with London to form the Third Coalition against France, Metternich worked to coordinate a coalition between Prussia and Austria. In August 1805 he induced Austria to join the alliance between Russia and Great Britain but was unable to persuade Prussia to do so. In October 1805, after Austrian generals were forced to surrender at Elchingen near Ulm, Frederick William was persuaded by Metternich and Hardenberg to meet with Alexander I in Berlin. These discussions led to durable relations between Metternich and Alexander.   In the short-term, Austria failed to secure firm Prussian support and was involved in a war with the French that could not be won. By November the French cavalry under General Joachim Murat (later, king of Naples, under Napoleon) had

Antoine-Jean Gros's equestrian portrait of the French general Joachim Murat, the leader of many successful cavalry campaigns under Napoleon. Murat was instrumental in the 1799 overthrow of the Directory, married Napoleon's sister Caroline, and in 1808 became king of Naples.

occupied Vienna, and on December 2, Napoleon won another stunning victory in the field against the 86,000 Russian and Austrian troops at Austerlitz. Emperor Francis was forced to surrender and to sign the Treaty of Pressburg on December 26. With this treaty Austria lost Venetia and all its other possessions in Italy. Napoleon and his generals hammered the Austrians at Ulm. As the new year opened, Metternich felt that he had aged 30 years and that old Europe was burning out; although much of the old order had been shattered, he believed, as he put it, "only from its ashes will a new order of existence arise."

In February 1806, it was decided that Metternich should be made the Austrian ambassador in Saint Petersburg (now the Soviet city of Leningrad), following his productive meeting with Alexander in Berlin. Metternich was overjoyed at this prospect, when Napoleon's destiny suddenly crossed that of the rising young Austrian diplomat. In some respects, a Trojan horse was about to enter Napoleon's camp. Napoleon demanded better Austrian repre-

A popular woodcut portrays Napoleon (seated, center) on the battlefield, after his December 1805 victory over the Austrians and Russians in the Battle of Austerlitz.

An anonymous painting depicts the meeting between the Holy Roman Emperor Francis II (later Francis I) and Napoleon, following the Battle of Austerlitz.

sentation in France and asked Talleyrand if he could not find another Kaunitz for the task. When Napoleon referred to the 18th-century Austrian statesman, his meaning was not vague. He was dropping hints that another Diplomatic Revolution was necessary to repair Franco-Austrian relations. Although Napoleon did not mention Metternich by name, his reference to the grandfather of the diplomatist's wife was sufficient to set certain gears in motion. When Metternich's name turned up, it was noted in Paris that the candidate had shown goodwill to the French representative while on assignment in Berlin. The appointment was confirmed. Metternich was delighted. He had reached the most decisive point in his career, and he knew it. Displaying his usual vanity in a letter to Eleonore, he boasted that he had surpassed all his colleagues. Metternich would now be face-to-face with the indomitable Napoleon as chief representative of the Habsburgs in Paris.

4

The Envoy

Metternich arrived in Paris on August 4. In his first meeting with Napoleon, he noted immediately the French emperor's immense insecurity. Standing in the middle of a large reception room, the emperor did not remove his hat. To Metternich such ill-mannered behavior was absurd rather than frightening. It struck the urbane diplomatist as "uncalled for pretentiousness indicating the parvenu. . . . His attempt to appear imposing had the effect of undermining in me the feeling of grandeur which one naturally associates with one before whom the world trembles."

There was, however, little doubt of the trembling in Vienna. Metternich had scarcely arrived in Paris when he heard of Napoleon's intention to establish a new Confederation of the Rhine. The Rhineland would thus be placed under French protective rule. Habsburg control in the southern and western German lands was coming to an end. In short, Francis would be faced with war if he did not accept the Confederation of the Rhine. In July, Napoleon's solution to the German question was accepted by 14 of the German states, including Baden, Bavaria, and Württemberg; Francis was left with little choice. On August 6, 1806, he decreed the end of the Holy Roman Empire and became solely the emperor of Austria as Francis I. Metternich was still his ambassador in Paris.

By force of circumstance Metternich had come into direct contact with Napoleon. No man could meet Napoleon in the day-to-day business of diplomacy and remain unchanged.
—E. L. WOODWARD
British historian

Francisco Goya's painting commemorates the Spanish resistance against Napoleon's 1808 invasion. Napoleon's concentration of troops in Spain created weaknesses in other parts of his European empire.

Metternich arrived in Paris in August 1806 as the city's Austrian ambassador. In this position, Metternich was able to work slowly and secretly toward the eventual downfall of the French dictator.

Napoleon was reshaping the German states with important future consequences for what had once been the Holy Roman Empire. Austria was looked upon by German nationalists as the leading power among them. For now, it seemed Austria had been cowed and was expected to be subservient to its new master. Forced to operate from such a powerless position, Metternich had little leverage with which to work, but he was determined to be equal to his task. Metternich's objective was simple: the survival of the Austrian Empire. But how best to accomplish it? Three wars had been fought to strengthen the Austrian position, and each one had further weakened the empire. Austria's subjugation meant that there was no longer a balance of power in Europe. Metternich knew that to restore it meant to offset the power of one nation by yoking together two or more weaker states. This also required that states within a coalition should not be permitted to overreach themselves, thus becoming yet another threat to security. At the start, Metternich would have to exercise stealth and his gift for observation. Gradually, he would have to deftly spring Austria from the trap. This was the situation that Metternich observed in his new political post. These were to be critical years for Napoleon with Metternich as intermediary. Few could foresee the complete reversal that would occur in less than a decade.

Metternich knew who held the trump cards and wrote to Gentz that Napoleon was "the only man in Europe who wills and acts." Thus, it was clear that the formulation of any successful policy would depend upon a careful and accurate assessment of Napoleon and his advisers. It did not take long to recognize certain weaknesses in Napoleon's position. As emperor, he was sensitive to any charge that his imperial title was that of an impostor. Such assertions did not affect the immense power Napoleon wielded so much as they wounded his pride.

Even the arrogant Napoleon realized, however, that emperors must be concerned with legitimacy, that which gave them the right to govern. For this purpose, he demonstrated that he could rely on the political device, the plebiscite, to obtain popular support within France. With regard to those people who found themselves absorbed into his empire, this innovative and democratic method was quite effective. To the Great Powers, plebiscites represented a form of democratic procedure that was dangerous in itself to monarchists and even more dangerous in the hands of Napoleon. The tyrant was using principles that appealed to the common masses against the royalists.

Despite his military prowess and political cunning, Napoleon was faced with a difficulty that is often particularly troublesome to kings and emperors. The birth of an heir to his throne was not forthcoming. Napoleon had been married to Josephine de Beauharnais since he first assumed command of the French army in Italy in March 1796. Though Josephine had two children by a previous marriage, she was now 43 years old, and Napoleon was growing concerned. She had not yet had a single child by him.

Metternich had an instinct for such delicate matters of state. For the moment, he had to wait, but an opening had been perceived. Meanwhile, Napoleon seized the initiative to launch another major offensive. Metternich was selected as Austrian am-

Napoleon married Josephine de Beauharnais in 1796. But by 1809 she had not borne him a son and was aging beyond her childbearing years, so Napoleon had the marriage annulled.

bassador to Paris a mere two months before the French defeated Prussia in the battles of Jena and Auerstädt on October 14, 1806. At Jena, the Prussians were caught by surprise and were overpowered by superior numbers; at Auerstädt the highly disciplined Prussian troops commanded by Scharnhorst were bested by the more flexible, fast-moving French, whose courage was bolstered by victory at Jena. The French occupied Berlin in the same month and Warsaw in November. As a consequence of Prussia's defeat, Napoleon seized a 1,850-mile area from territory controlled by Austria, Prussia, and Russia, territory that once had been Poland. From it he created the Grand Duchy of Warsaw by the summer of 1807. Under the Treaty of Tilsit, Prussia was punished heavily by Napoleon. As Napoleon and Alexander agreed that Prussia would lose territory and thus half its population, the Prussian king stood nearby in a rainstorm, helpless to affect the negotiations. Napoleon's military strength and territorial holdings were at their peak. Frederick William's kingdom underwent the indignity of being occupied by French troops. As for Rus-

Napoleon supervises the battle formation of his troops at the Battle of Jena, where he defeated the Prussians, the last group to join the Third Coalition against him.

sia, according to the historian J. G. Lockhart, "Napoleon had given Alexander a lesson in war at Austerlitz; he gave him a lesson in diplomacy at Tilsit." In stark contrast to his treatment of Prussia, Napoleon reached an agreement with Alexander I that startled many observers. Russia and France came to an understanding based on the new political realities introduced by Napoleon and divided Europe between them. They also concluded a secret alliance, with Russia agreeing to support the Continental Blockade that Napoleon had announced from Berlin in November 1806. The emperor of the French had long wanted to call a halt to British shipping to and from Russia.

England and France were now engaged in a war for commercial supremacy. The economic conflict began with an English embargo on French and Dutch trade in 1803. Three years later the British tried to blockade the continent, and the Berlin Decree in November was Napoleon's response. In it Napoleon articulated his Continental System that threatened to turn the struggle against Great Britain into a war on trade, literally laying siege to the British economy. All ports within Napoleon's control were closed to the British. These measures were intensified when the Warsaw Decrees were proclaimed in January 1807 and the British counter-

Following the October 1806 battles of Jena and Auerstadt, Napoleon marched into and occupied Berlin. In the following month, he seized Warsaw.

After Napoleon defeated Austria, Prussia, and Russia, a surprise agreement was reached between the French dictator and the Russian tsar. At the July 1807 meetings at Tilsit, Napoleon (left) and Alexander I divided the conquered territories between them.

attacked with the Orders in Council. Napoleon then presented the Milan Decree, which interdicted all shipping that observed the British Orders. Napoleon's Continental System relied upon continued goodwill between France and Russia. Without it there would be tremendous holes in any effective blockade.

All of this was noted by the Austrian ambassador in France. While Napoleon was engaged in an ever widening struggle for preeminence, Metternich established relations with a small number of Frenchmen in Paris. His two most important relationships were with Talleyrand, former minister of foreign affairs and still in the service of Napoleon, and the former Jacobin Joseph Fouché, the minister of police in Paris until 1802. Metternich gathered information from them that revealed court gossip. He kept tabs on popular opinion while continuing to assess the Austrian position.

During these years Metternich's memoirs reveal that he also developed a grudging respect for what he called "Napoleon's practical mind" and "his undoubted genius." "Had Napoleon confined his plans to the preservation of what the Republic had conquered," Metternich wrote, "he would have greatly increased his popularity; his warlike temperament carried him much farther." In February 1808,

French troops were sent into Spain. It was a turning point in the fortunes of Napoleon.

Within three months significant resistance to the French occupation began with a revolt in Madrid on May 2, celebrated by Spanish patriots as the *Dos de Mayo* and commemorated in works by the 19th-century Spanish painter Francisco Goya. That same month Napoleon's brother, Joseph, who had been king in Naples, was made king of Spain — an outrage to the Spanish people. For the first time Napoleon was challenging a people motivated to fight by intense patriotism. The force that he had harnessed so well in France was the same one that stood in his way in Spain. Because the Continental System also depended upon the control of Spanish ports, valuable forces were committed in Spain that made Napoleon vulnerable in other areas of Europe. Napoleon's potential weakness made itself evident to the Austrian minister of foreign affairs, Count Johann Philipp Karl Joseph Stadion, who wished to take advantage of this misadventure in Spain to attack Napoleon by surprise. From his position in Paris, Metternich did nothing to dissuade him. Stadion was a nationalist who wanted to build resistance to the occupier. Of course, Metternich did all he could to appease the imperious conqueror on the surface while secretly cooperating with Stadion. The young ambassador had to hold his tongue whenever Napoleon told his sister, Caroline Murat, to "entertain this simpleton," at social gatherings, before brusquely walking off.

Stadion had succeeded the conservative and cautious Count Ludwig Cobenzl as minister of foreign affairs in 1805 and hoped to engineer a more dynamic foreign policy. Cobenzl, though opposed to war, had entered the Third Coalition with Great Britain and Russia out of a sense of desperation. His predecessor, Baron Thugut, had attempted to tackle Napoleon alone, a policy that led to Austrian defeat in 1800 at the Battle of Marengo and surrender in 1801. Austria then lost Belgium, Northern Italy, and the left bank of the Rhine, when the Second Coalition was crushed.

Charles-Maurice de Talleyrand, French statesman and diplomat under Napoleon, feared the expansionist policies of his emperor. He befriended Metternich in Paris and argued successfully for the reinstatement of the Bourbon monarchy after Napoleon's downfall.

From his ambassadorship in the remote Russian capital, Metternich had supported Cobenzl and the Third Coalition. He was convinced that a successful coalition against Napoleon required close cooperation with Russia and full support from Prussia. Without these assurances the coalition could only fail. The 1805 defeat that resulted was decisive, and it would take longer to recover from this enormous setback than even Metternich could foresee.

One favorable outcome for Austria of the military and diplomatic disasters in 1805 was that Stadion was appointed minister of foreign affairs and Metternich was made Austrian ambassador to France. While based in France, Metternich became increasingly aware of the use of propaganda as a political weapon. He was forced to learn the value of manipulating public opinion from Napoleon — his hated adversary in whose court he served. Could not the forces of German nationalism be harnessed to work for Austrian purposes as well as those of Napoleon? Napoleon was quite aware that German nationalism presented a problem to his empire. He explained to Metternich his contempt for those princes of the new Confederation of the Rhine who still dreamed about restoring the old German Reich that existed under the Holy Roman Empire. According to Metternich, Napoleon told spokesmen for this position, "In Germany the small people want to be protected against the great people; the great wish to govern according to their own fancy; now, as I only want from the federation men and money, and as it is the great people and not the small who can provide me with both, I leave the former alone in peace, and the second have only to settle themselves as best they may!"

After Napoleon committed his armies in Spain, Metternich urged Stadion to launch a people's war, using a militia, under the leadership of the Austrian emperor. In the meantime, the general Archduke Charles could prepare the army to battle the French once more. It was a policy that could prove effective in bringing Prussia back into the Austrian camp. In addition, Metternich had the added advantage of cooperation from Talleyrand, then grand chamberlain of the empire, who was secretly opposed to Napoleon's dangerous expansionist policies.

The French invasion of Spain also gave encouragement to Talleyrand, an aristocrat, who, like Metternich, was resentful of Napoleon and increasingly determined to undermine his position. As Napoleon's visions of domination became ever more clear, Talleyrand and Metternich began to share a common concern about the emperor of the French. At home Napoleon had already done away with the Tribunate, the legislative section of the Consulate, thus removing virtually all restraints on his power. When from September 27 until October 14, 1808, Tsar Alexander and Napoleon met at Erfurt (now in East Germany) to discuss the possible division of the Turkish Empire, Talleyrand went so far as to advise the Russian tsar to resist his emperor. Such advice could have been considered treasonous. Tal-

Between September 27 and October 24, 1808, Napoleon (center) and other dignitaries convened at Erfurt to decide the fate of the Turkish empire. These meetings proved unsuccessful.

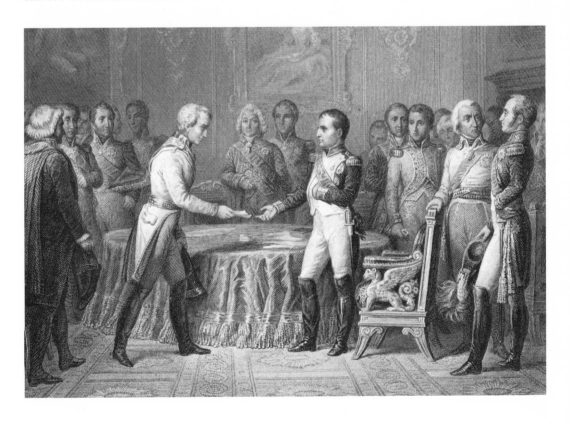

A secret Tyrolean armament workshop. The Tyroleans, under the leadership of Andreas Hofer, rose up against Napoleon, who had annexed their province to the Bavarians in 1805. Tyrol was finally returned to Austria in 1815.

leyrand subsequently let Metternich be aware of this deed. Metternich, in turn, quickly informed Stadion that relations between Russia and France were not all that they appeared to be. These negotiations were not nearly as successful as the previous Treaty of Tilsit. Eventually, the tsar fancied that only Russia, under his leadership, could save Europe from the Napoleonic scourge. By 1811, Alexander found these words for Napoleon, "the infernal being . . . becomes from day to day more abominable."

Acting on Metternich's advice to initiate a popular uprising against Napoleon, Stadion exploited popular discontent in the Tyrol against the territory's annexation by Bavaria in 1805. In Vienna the war party (those favoring active military policy) made contact with Tyrolean patriots led by Andreas Hofer, hoping to coordinate their efforts. When Napoleon decided to take Tyrolean conscripts into his army, the alliance between the Viennese party and the patriots was accepted. A popular insurrection in the Tyrol would coincide with an Austrian declaration of war on France. Once again, the Austrians gallantly raised the sword against Napoleon.

In a letter dated April 3, 1809, Metternich made his feelings clear to Stadion about the strategy agreed upon: "The French government does not hide its intentions: let us profit from them. In a word, let us fight the enemy with his own weapons." Metternich continued: "We are, for the first time for some years, strong in ourselves, let us take advantage of our strength, and never forget that the year 1809 is . . . the first of a new era."

Austria declared war six days after Metternich wrote this letter to Stadion. Two days later the ambassador wrote again to the minister of foreign affairs, explaining that time had strengthened Austria's position:

> The war against Austria in 1805 was unpopular in France; that of 1809 is still more so. The Treasury of the state was then full, now it is emptied in a great measure by the Spanish war. Napoleon then employed his whole army; it was composed of old regiments intoxicated by former successes. . . . The Head of the old German Empire in 1805, had only enemies in Germany. Now the cause of Austria is that of all nations up to the bank of the Rhine. . . . Our position is, therefore, no doubt better; it is far beyond what the boldest wishes could have formerly imagined. If we succumb, it will only be from our own fault or from delay."

During April, as Austria set its plot in motion, Metternich did not elude the serious consequences that accompanied renewed hostilities. Two French ambassadors were jailed in Hungary by the Austrians. In retaliation Metternich was seized and placed under arrest. Napoleon kept him captive until the Austrian war of resistance was smashed.

As it turned out, Metternich's analysis proved faulty and his prediction wildly inaccurate. Austria succumbed once more to Napoleon's Grande Armée. On May 12, Napoleon's forces captured Vienna after first overcoming heavy resistance. He was wounded at Eckmühl and was blocked by Archduke Charles at the Battle of Aspern, or Essling. Strangely, however, it was the failure of the Austrian armed forces that brought Metternich to the Austrian Foreign Office.

After being brought in June to Vienna under mil-

The key to success in diplomacy was freedom of action, not formal relationships. This was the basis of Metternich's diplomacy throughout his life.
—HENRY KISSINGER
American secretary of state

Horace Vernet's painting glorifies Napoleon's command of his troops at the Battle of Wagram. Metternich had miscalculated the strength of the French *Grand Armée*, and once again Napoleon crushed the Austrian armed forces.

itary guard, Metternich was released in July in exchange for the two Frenchmen held prisoner by the Austrians. In a battle that was observed at close range by both Metternich and Emperor Francis, Napoleon's commanders and their remarkable war machine demonstrated their superiority once more. "We will have much to retrieve," Francis said. A French victory at the Battle of Wagram on July 5–6, 1809, forced Stadion to submit his resignation.

Stadion resigned because he assumed that his open dislike for Napoleon would guarantee a harsh settlement for Austria. Metternich wanted to postpone taking action because he did not wish to be associated directly with a defeat. It was well understood in the Austrian court that Metternich was in the best position to negotiate with Napoleon and

finally, on August 4, Metternich was appointed conference minister and minister of state. He was then appointed minister of the imperial household and of foreign affairs on October 8. Francis put his name to the treaty Napoleon dictated without Metternich having anything to say about the terms.

The Treaty of Schönbrunn, signed in Vienna on October 14, 1809, was indeed harsh. It deprived Austria of its Polish territory in Galicia, including the city of Cracow. In Germany, the district around the Inn River, Berchtesgaden, and Salzburg was ceded to Bavaria. Around the coast of the Adriatic, the Austrian provinces of Carinthia, Croatia (now part of Yugoslavia), and Carniola (one of the Illyrian provinces, now part of Yugoslavia) were lost as well. The key ports of Fiume and Trieste in Italy were joined with the newly formed Illyrian provinces as part of Napoleon's empire, and Trentino was added to the kingdom of Italy. In spite of its weakened finances, Austria was forced to pay an indemnity. The Austrian army was limited to 150,000 men, and as a final slap in the face, Austria was required to join the Continental System.

On October 14, 1809, Emperor Francis I signed a treaty with Napoleon at the Schönbrunn Palace in Vienna. The emperor agreed to the harsh terms of the treaty without consulting his minister of foreign affairs, Metternich.

5

The Lion in the Net

Y ou are indeed young," Napoleon said to the new Austrian minister of foreign affairs, "to represent the oldest monarchy in Europe." Metternich replied, "Sire, my age is the same as Your Majesty's at Austerlitz." At age 36, he assumed his country's highest diplomatic post at the very moment when the Habsburgs' prospects were extremely dismal. Before accepting the appointment as minister of the imperial household and of foreign affairs, Metternich reported to his emperor just how much the Austrian defeat at Wagram had altered his position. Metternich's bold hopes for a new era, starting in 1809, had tumbled down. While negotiations were still in progress, Metternich explained to Francis "that we shall find our safety only by accommodating ourselves to the triumphant system of France. . . . My principles are unchangeable, but to necessity we must yield." The future did not look bright but it still had to be considered in the gray light of the present. "From the day when peace is signed," Metternich continued, "we must confine our system to tacking, and turning, and flattering." Only in this manner could Austria survive "till the day of general deliverance."

Austria could not act independently. Efforts to form an effective coalition had collapsed, and the

> *Metternich, on his part, never liked Napoleon. He saw him as the incarnation of the Revolution, the enemy of Europe, and a crowned vulgarian.*
> —J. G. LOCKHART
> American historian

At the age of 36, Metternich was appointed Austrian minister of the imperial household and of foreign affairs. At this time Napoleon's power appeared invincible and Metternich reevaluated his long-term plans for ridding Europe of the French emperor's tyrannical control.

attempt to coordinate a popular uprising with Austrian help had failed. German liberation seemed to have been stamped out. Andreas Hofer led the peasants of the Tyrol to early victories, but he was captured by the French in 1810, court-martialed, and shot. Every policy that the Austrians pursued had ended in failure; and, in effect, the Habsburg Empire was now powerless against Napoleon, who dominated Europe.

In clear, direct language Metternich did not spare Francis the truth. As long as the present policy of France and Russia remained the same, there was little that could be done. Austria had to wait for Russia to decide to become a pivotal member of a coalition. "Without the assistance of Russia," the foreign minister wrote, "opposition to the universal pressure is not to be thought of. That vacillating court will awake more quickly if it finds that nothing more is to be gained by its miserable policy." "For us," continued Metternich, "there remains but one expedient, to increase our strength for better days, to work out our preservation by gentle means, without looking back upon our former course."

Metternich realized Austria's future hinged on two crucial issues: the outcome of the Continental System and how long harmony would prevail between France and Russia. The economic war of attrition between Great Britain and France raged on inconclusively. There was little that Austria could do to alter the outcome of that struggle.

By finding a way to preserve Austria "by gentle means," perhaps, Metternich thought, a wedge could be driven between France and Russia. Because of their childlessness, the emperor and empress were about to be divorced. Napoleon's frustration and anxiety concerning his need for a legitimate heir to his throne was the talk of the court. The foreign minister was in Vienna when he heard of Napoleon's plan to marry Tsar Alexander's sister Anna. Such a marriage would encourage closer French relations with Russia and give Napoleon the added security that he sought for the throne. If Napoleon found a way to perpetuate his

line, Austria could remain subjugated for a long time to come. To Metternich's great relief, news arrived that the tsar had turned down Napoleon's proposal on the grounds that his 16-year-old sister was too young for marriage.

At last, Metternich was given his chance to make a serious impact on this delicate matter, thus changing Napoleon's — and Europe's — future. In his search for a new wife, Napoleon turned to Austria. Metternich at once suggested Archduchess Marie Louise, the 18-year-old daughter of the Austrian emperor, as the most suitable partner for Napoleon. Metternich's wife, Eleonore, who had remained in Paris, was most helpful in championing the proposed political partnership. Knowledgeable about both romantic and diplomatic affairs of state, she had the support of Talleyrand. At this time, Talleyrand was continuing good relations with Austria. This suggestion met even with Josephine's approval. In February 1810, Napoleon made his final

After the annulment of his marriage to Josephine in 1809, Napoleon married the Archduchess Marie-Louise, the daughter of Emperor Francis I. The marriage placed Austria in a more favorable diplomatic position with Napoleon.

decision to marry the Habsburg princess, and it was approved by her father. Marie Louise was married by proxy in the Chapel of the Hofburg on March 11 and two days later left for France, conducted by Metternich, to meet her new husband.

On April 2 the 18-year-old empress celebrated her marriage once more in the Louvre in Paris. A few months later, she became pregnant, and the heir to the throne of Napoleon I was born on March 20, 1811. On the surface, a happier dynastic marriage could not have been realized. The arrival of Napoleon II appeared to satisfy all parties. With the child's birth it appeared that fortune had been delivered to Austria. Napoleon had his desired legitimate heir, and Austria had much improved its political position on the Continent. There still remained another troubling issue, however. Napoleon was still regarded as a pretender — an illegitimate usurper. He had improved his status, but it was still dependent upon his ability to control territory and expand the empire he commanded. By 1812, Napoleon was once more meddling furiously in the international situation in his struggle for unquestioned supremacy. He had at his disposal more than 600,000 troops in April 1812.

Napoleon was at the apex of his power, having established his Grand Empire between 1810 and 1811. The Austrian foreign minister was wrong about Napoleon's character in 1809. But this time his instincts were correct: "That Napoleon, in his lust of power on the European continent, had already overstepped the limits of the possible — of this I had not the slightest doubt. I foresaw that neither he nor his undertakings would escape the consequence of rashness and extravagance."

Although he prided himself on his insight, Metternich could not be sure of when or how these limits would present themselves. Yet Metternich's adversary had reason to gloat. To be sure, the Continental System had not crushed Britain, but it had helped create a financial crisis there. The gears of Great Britain's Industrial Revolution were being slowed as strikes and riots erupted among mill workers and factory workers in the large cities. Portugal, which briefly escaped Napoleon's tyranny, was reconquered. On the Iberian Peninsula the only holdouts were at Lisbon and Cadiz. The French position in Italy never seemed more secure, and Russia was involved in an inconclusive war with Turkey over Serbia (now part of Yugoslavia).

Metternich had played a brilliant gambit for his emperor. Because of the solution Austria was able to devise for Napoleon's dilemma, a sort of diplomatic reversal began to occur. The wedge was being driven in. The tsar of Russia was displeased about Napoleon's marriage to the Habsburg archduchess. For his part, Napoleon was frustrated by the Russian's inability to enforce his blockade against British shipping. Furthermore, the tsar had shown an avid interest in Poland since 1809. Then, on April 8, 1812, Alexander demanded that French forces withdraw from Prussia. Napoleon rejected this ultimatum and two months later used it as a pretext for war. During a blazing summer, beginning on June 24 a combined army of 20 nations, totaling 650,000 men and speaking 12 languages, marched and galloped into Russia. No more than 200,000 men from this invasion force were Frenchmen. Napoleon's Grande Armée could not call on the Russian peasants for support. The peasantry met the invaders with a scorched-earth policy. Wherever the invaders went, they discovered great swaths of burned crops and charred, smoking huts. Nothing was left to conquer but the burning earth.

Metternich made an agreement with Napoleon whereby only 30,000 Austrian soldiers and 1 general would accompany the emperor on his Russian adventure. Even though Austrian soldiers were included among Napoleon's forces in Russia, Metternich was determined to keep Austria out of a military entanglement. In October 1810 he returned to Vienna from Paris and successfully prevented pro-Russian factions from shifting the Habsburg court to Alexander's side. He assured the tsar that Austria would be an "active friend" and not an "enemy in war" on the battlefield. The advice he gave

Shortly after her marriage to Napoleon, Marie-Louise bore him a son. Napoleon II fulfilled his father's obsessive desire to leave behind a legitimate heir to his throne.

to Francis that year was almost a sacred principle to Metternich: "In a war between France and Russia, Austria must take a position on the flank which will ensure a decisive importance for her opinions during the war, and at the end of it."

Russian armies did not actually meet the enemy until September, when the Russian general Prince Mikhail Ilarionovich Kutuzov engaged Napoleon in the Battle of Borodino. The Russians lost a staggering 45,000 men, and the battle ended in a stalemate. Kutuzov fought at Austerlitz, where he was wounded. He was also battle-hardened, having been commander in chief of Russian forces against the Turks until Napoleon's invasion of Russia. Seven days later, on September 14, Napoleon's vast army entered Moscow. Already behind in his military timetable, Napoleon was prepared to negotiate with

Russian Field Marshal Mikhail Ilarionovich Kutuzov (1745–1813), prince of Smolensk, led the Russians in their defense against Napoleon's 1812 invasion of their homeland.

Alexander and, if necessary, quarter his army in Moscow. The tsar, however, did not comply with Napoleon's expectations. Again, there was no prize for Napoleon, for the city was put to the torch by the Russians. Hoping to live comfortably on what they could plunder from the Russian capital, Napoleon's army saw provisions go up in flames and decided to withdraw. Russian forces to the south, led by Kutuzov, forced him to retreat by the same route that had been scorched during the summer invasion — through Smolensk, of which Kutuzov was prince. There would be meager food and supplies for a weary army. By November heavy snows fell; intense cold attacked Napoleon's men. Only 100,000 men from his original army of 650,000 survived the Russian winter. Napoleon abandoned Russia when he received word of conspiracy against him in Paris. The Russians forced him to fight his way out. Marshal Ney courageously defended the retreating column. Napoleon arrived in the French capital on December 18, 1812, a week before Christmas. In their prolonged misery, his troops celebrated the birth of the Christian savior in frozen Russia.

Metternich understood the potential impact of Napoleon's mistakes. He had maintained good relations with the Russians without giving in completely to their wishes. Lines of communication were kept open with the Prussians during this time. Napoleon himself was never easy to predict. By December, however, there was enough information to guess that even Napoleon's huge ego must have been affected by the catastrophe in Russia. Metternich devised a diplomatic maneuver that was designed to reveal the French emperor's intentions.

Metternich planned to mediate among the nations for a general European peace. But he had to extricate Austria from its dependence on France. To do so, he needed to guarantee his country mobility. In order for his long-range plans to proceed, he knew that freedom from certain alliances was essential. An envoy went to Napoleon on Metternich's orders. He was to sound out the emperor regarding whether Austrian mediation in the Russo-French conflict

Tsar Alexander I had shifted his alliance from Austria to France; nevertheless, he refused to cooperate with Napoleon after the *Grande Armée* marched into Moscow. Political ties between the two nations were finally destroyed.

would be acceptable to him. Metternich's position was bolstered when he learned that Napoleon needed troops, and he was only too eager to appear helpful to him. The emperor wanted to reinvade Russia in the spring and informed the Austrian ambassador. This hint of weakness on the French side also strengthened Metternich's emerging role as mediator.

Without guaranteeing Napoleon the use of Austrian forces, the foreign minister was content to let Napoleon encourage an Austrian military buildup. An armistice was agreed to between Russia and Austria on January 30, 1813. Secretly, the 30,000 Austrians in Russia were permitted to back off before the Russian armies. The Prussians did the same, withdrawing to Galicia and halting there. This action stemmed from the Convention of Tauroggen in December 1812 between Russian and Prussian forces, allowing the Prussians to quietly fall back before the Russians. Tauroggen stood the Prussians on their feet to resist Napolean and spurred Prussian patriotism. Then, on February 28, Russia and Prussia agreed to the Treaty of Kalisch. The ground for cooperation between these two states involved their respective interests in Poland and Saxony, but this treaty did nothing to prevent Napoleon from taking to the field again. Its primary outcome was the Prussian nationalist War of Liberation (*Befreiungskrieg*) against the French. Two victories in May at Lützen, against Prussia, and Bautzen, against Russia, raised Napoleon's prestige and threatened Metternich's role as arbiter. Secretly, Metternich applauded this new coalition. Publicly, he maintained friendly relations with France. To establish Austrian independence and to exercise maximum influence were his objectives. His chance came in June when Napoleon concluded the Armistice of Pläzwitz. French victories had been costly, and Napoleon's troops were exhausted. His need to buy time favored Metternich.

There was still a war party in Vienna headed by the former foreign minister, Stadion. But Francis, ever cautious, was not ready to go to war again after doing so five times against Napoleon. The memory of defeat was still too vivid, and Metternich could not afford to lose his emperor's support. The armistice at Pläzwitz was scheduled to last from June 4 until July 20, 1813, and Metternich took full advantage of the time he was given.

Metternich met with the tsar in June. Alexander neither trusted Metternich's motives nor wished to appease Napoleon. In June, Metternich and the tsar reached an understanding, resulting in the Treaty of Reichenbach, concluded by Austria, Russia, and Prussia on June 27. This agreement proposed the end of the Grand Duchy of Warsaw, a resettlement of the territory lost by Prussia, and the return of

Illyria (Illyrian provinces) to Austria; Hamburg and Lübeck were to revert to their status of free cities once more. Finally, French military control of the Confederation of the Rhine was to be ended. These terms were moderate, and nothing really was promised to Napoleon if he agreed to them. The entire proposition depended upon Napoleon's acceptance. Before a pen was lifted to scratch signatures on this treaty, Metternich obtained Russian and Prussian approval to proceed to Dresden, as mediator, for a consultation with Napoleon. They met as planned on June 26, 1813. Both the diplomat and the emperor were strong-willed, with unshakable confidence in their own beliefs.

Metternich appealed to Napoleon's almost limitless sense of his own importance: "The fate of Europe, her future and yours, all lie in your hands. Between Europe and the aims you have hitherto pursued there is absolute contradiction. The world

Napoleon defeated the Prussians at the Battle of Lützen in May 1813. For the moment he appeared victorious in the Prussian nationalist war of liberation against France.

requires peace; you must reduce your power within bounds compatible with the general tranquility, or you will fall in the contest. Today you can yet conclude peace; tomorrow it may be too late."

Napoleon's reply was sharp: "Do they want me to degrade myself? Never! I shall know how to die; but I shall not yield one handbreadth of soil. Your sovereigns, born to the throne, may be beaten twenty times, and still go back to their palaces; that cannot I — the child of fortune; my reign will not outlast the day when I have ceased to be strong, and therefore to be feared."

Despite this explosive reaction, Napoleon agreed to continue with the negotiation. Metternich ultimately convinced Napoleon to accept an extension of the armistice until August 10. Metternich was concerned that Napoleon would seek war if Austria refused to cooperate with him any longer. The French emperor boasted of his recent victories at Lützen and Bautzen. Metternich was quick to remind him about the logic of numbers and his overwhelming losses in Russia: "Your majesty has the feeling that you are absolutely necessary to the nation; but is not the nation also necessary to you? And if this juvenile army that you levied but yesterday should be swept away, what then?"

At these remarks, according to Metternich, Napoleon turned pale and was overcome with rage, but quickly recovered. "The French," he answered, "cannot complain of me; to spare them, I have sacrificed the Germans and the Poles. I have lost in the campaign of Moscow three hundred thousand men, and there were not more than thirty thousand Frenchmen among them."

"You forget, sire," Metternich explained, "that you are speaking to a German."

Metternich and Napoleon had met for the last time. Napoleon wondered if his marriage to the archduchess of Austria meant anything at all to the emperor of Austria, and Metternich responded that the emperor knew nothing but his duty. The two antagonists had explained their position; each man was convinced that he was right. The only alter-

> *Few people understand how much advantage can be taken of cunning people; for my part I have never been afraid of them provided they have intelligence. The only adversary it is difficult to vanquish is the perfectly honest man.*
> —PRINCE METTERNICH

native was war. After their interview Metternich is said to have remarked to a member of Napoleon's staff, "Your emperor is a lost man."

Gradually the threads of the coalition were drawn together through previous agreements; by the terms of the Treaty of Kalisch, Prussia could not conduct negotiations to which Russia was not also a party. According to the Treaty of Reichenbach, Russia could not negotiate agreements without Great Britain. At a conference at Prague, Metternich gave the French an ultimatum. A treaty would have to be signed by August 10, or Austria would have no choice but to declare war.

Time ran out for the French, and Austria went to war. Austria joined the Last Coalition against Napoleon on August 11, 1813. This was the Grand Alliance aimed at slaying the Napoleonic dragon. Two months later, on October 16, the famous "Battle of the Nations," or the Battle of Leipzig, forced Napoleon to withdraw his new army behind the safety of the Rhine after losing 38,000 men. Metternich's diplomacy had not only maneuvered Napoleon into an uncompromising position; it also brought Austria into a coalition and called forth a people's war. Patient and practical diplomacy had placed Austria in an independent position for the first time in more than a decade. In the long run, the military success in the Battle of the Nations increased nationalist fervor in central Europe against France. Guided by the principle of the balance of power, Metternich quickly recognized that the rapid westward advance of the Russian armies must be checked. Accordingly, in November, Metternich made another offer of peace to Napoleon that was so generous that it aroused a protest from the British government. Napoleon again refused, but he also believed that he had until spring to regroup his army. In this he was mistaken. Given the military and political circumstances, Metternich was not prepared to wait. An Austrian offensive led by Karl Philipp, prince of Schwarzenberg, commenced on December 13, 1813. In January a Prussian army under Marshal Gebhard Leberecht von Blücher also

Metternich (left) needed to maintain the support of Emperor Francis I (right), who had not forgotten his five bitter defeats by Napoleon. Metternich thus moved cautiously forward with negotiations among Austria, Russia, and Prussia.

crossed the Rhine. Napoleon's imperialism had finally provoked a widespread German national spirit, and now it would help to crush the French. Metternich had indeed helped to support a cause that would haunt him later, but for the moment the forces of German nationalism furthered his own cause. The allied forces marched quickly and triumphantly through France. Napoleon was unable to hold off the Austrians and Prussians. At last the master of war found himself stymied. Metternich keenly watched allied forces as they closed in on Paris.

In January 1814 representatives of the Big Four met near the town of Châtillon in France. Castlereagh insisted at the subsequent Congress of Châtillon that France should be forced back to its boundaries of 1792, the *anciennes limites*. The Congress convened on February 6, five days after Blücher defeated Napoleon at the Battle of La Rothière.

On March 9, Austria, Great Britain, Prussia, and

With Napoleon's loss of Russia as an ally and his defeat at the Battle of Leipzig in October 1813, allied forces marched easily through France and took Paris in March 1814.

Russia signed the Treaty of Chaumont in Dijon, France, pledging that no separate treaties would be signed with the French. Peace would be decided as a cooperative effort by all the coalition's members. An agreement of its magnitude had never occurred in history before. It had taken more than 20 years to forge an effective coalition against France. The Treaty of Chaumont guaranteed the existence of the coalition for the next 20 years. (As compared with alliances, coalitions are made between several nations, are organized around a certain principle, such as the balance of power. Over time, alliances far outnumber coalitions.)

A treaty with France, the First Peace of Paris, was concluded on May 30, 1814, between Great Britain, Russia, Austria, and Prussia. Castlereagh of Britain wanted the agreement to be free "of anything bearing upon it the character of particular distrust." Having reserved the more general questions of European security for a larger Congress to be held in Vienna in the autumn of 1814, it had been much easier to negotiate peace with France. Metternich did not dwell on his past success. The Austrian army was not alone in France; Russian and Prussian troops also occupied Paris. Much remained to be done. Preliminary meetings for the scheduled Congress of Vienna were held in London during June and July, and Metternich remained there until an opening day was set for the Congress. It was scheduled to begin on October 1, and Metternich returned to Vienna to begin with the early preparations as convener.

He arrived in the Austrian capital on July 19, 1814, and was greeted as a triumphant hero by an orchestra playing the "Prometheus Overture" by Ludwig van Beethoven, who had lived in Vienna and had once been an admirer of Napoleon. A choir sang a cantata, opening with the lines "Hail to thee, great Prince, whose prudent wisdom guided the royal course." It closed with the following — "History holds thee up to posterity as a Model among Great Men."

6

"The Rock of Order"

Metternich was not deceived by his reception as a hero in Vienna. His vanity was great, but not greater than his intelligence. Not distracted by this rare show of public praise, the foreign minister focused on critical questions still to be answered before a more secure peace could be declared. Political stability in Europe would not be achieved until solutions were reached for the future of the Germans, the Italians, and the Poles — issues that continued to threaten the new equilibrium established by the Coalition against Napoleon. The preliminary conferences held in London during the summer of 1814 revealed the difficulty in preserving the unity demonstrated at Chaumont. The First Treaty of Paris was only a beginning.

Reservations about the prospects for cooperation and unity at the Congress of Vienna were evident. Even before the Congress opened, Metternich lost his composure with Alexander concerning the question of Poland. He bluntly informed the tsar that Austria was just as able to create an independent Polish state as Russia. The tsar, knowing that his troops already occupied Poland, shouted at Metternich: "You are the only man in Austria who would dare to oppose me in such rebellious terms." And so it was; the foreign minister who had survived the onslaughts of Napoleon was now ready to stand

Metternich savored the incense of adulation with the contentment of one who had never doubted his right to be numbered among the illustrious.
—ALAN PALMER
Metternich biographer,
on Metternich's 1814
return to Vienna

Second Viscount Robert Stewart Castlereagh (1769–1822), Britain's foreign minister, conceived of the Concert of Europe, a plan whereby the major European powers continued to meet after 1818 to discuss the general well-being of their continent.

against Alexander. He was not prepared to see either Russia or France dominate central Europe.

After the initial altercation with Alexander, Metternich resolved to stall for time. Hoping to allow tensions to dissipate, he immersed himself in social events during the first months of the Congress. Even his close friend and secretary, Friedrich von Gentz, noted his seeming indifference to this important political question. Nonetheless, not a single issue from Metternich's "Instructions" of 1801 was omitted from the agenda at the Congress. His assertions regarding "the fickle character of the Russian Emperor," Poland, Prussia, Saxony, and "the restoration of the European balance of power" became firmly wedged into the dialogues the Congress would hold.

Metternich was sure that no power by itself could maintain the peace. A harmonious coalition had defeated Napoleon, and harmony would be vital to protecting the fruits of victory. A balance of power in central Europe was necessary for Austria above all, it seemed to Metternich.

Metternich returned to Vienna a hero in July 1814, after the defeat of Napoleon and the signing of the First Peace of Paris treaty the previous May.

Many years later he stated that "political bodies . . . only enjoy true independence when they are surrounded by sufficient strength to guarantee their well-being." He wanted Austria to provide that strength in central Europe. German and Italian affairs should naturally be controlled by Austria, he thought. Metternich had to persuasively depict the Austrian position as being in the interests of all Europe. In addition, Austrian territorial claims could not appear to endanger Austria's legitimacy as a state. If this occurred it could easily ruin both Austrian security and the balance of power toward which he was striving. When Metternich met with Castlereagh in London, prior to the Congress, he found the British foreign secretary largely in agreement with him.

Diplomats at the Congress, by and large, were practical. Tsar Alexander was the principal exception. Having worked so long to clarify the principles involved in the negotiations, Metternich now pursued them with vigor.

Practicality sometimes clashed with higher principles. According to Koch, Metternich's former teacher, "ambitious projects of conquerors" must be blocked in order to "sacrifice . . . personal views to the general welfare. . . ." But there were those at the Congress whose "ambitious projects" were in plain view. Some powers appeared to be guided by the concepts set forth by 15th-century Italian statesman Nicoló Machiavelli in *The Prince*. Gentz reports that ruthless self-interest, rather than idealism, prevailed at the Congress. He wrote that phrases such as " 'reconstruction of social order,' a 'lasting peace founded on a great division of strength'. . . were uttered to tranquilize the people. . . but the real purpose was to divide the . . . spoils taken from the vanquished."

It became increasingly clear that Metternich assigned too great a role to Austria in maintaining the balance. Also, the principle of legitimacy was not so easily applied to all the territorial adjustments necessitated by the war's end.

To maintain the upper hand in the German and Italian states Metternich gave up the Netherlands.

This was a wise move because the Netherlands were distant from the center of Habsburg power and could not be connected directly to Austrian territory. British concerns about securing ports on the English Channel, however, dictated the need for a strong state in the Netherlands as a check on France. There was general agreement that France should be guarded, as a precaution, on all its boundaries. This agreement gave the diplomats ample room for compromise. Metternich had no trouble satisfying Castlereagh's interest in protecting the English Channel. Castlereagh reciprocated by recognizing Metternich's wish to oversee the eastern frontier of France and Austria's southern boundary in Italy. In return for surrendering its long-standing interests in the Netherlands, Austria was compensated with Lombardy and Venetia in northern Italy and Dalmatia (part of Yugoslavia) on the Adriatic coast. After the Polish issue was settled, Austria recovered Galacia as well as the Illyrian provinces. Prussia was granted the Rhineland, including the Ruhr and the Saar valleys, as a further check on France.

Indeed, German nationalism had been essential to overthrowing Napoleon, but the Congress did not reflect this growing desire for a unified German state. Rather, Metternich made certain that Austria came to be the leading power among the members of the confederation until its abolition by Prussia in 1867. After his devastating victories in 1806, Napoleon himself paved the way for this arrangement by consolidating 300 German states from the Holy Roman Empire into the 38 states of the Confederation of the Rhine. His administrative changes in the region imposed a more or less French system on these states. Russia was granted the Prussian holdings in Poland, but Prussia was compensated for this by control of Danzig (now Gdansk) and much of Saxony. British interests were served by uniting the former Austrian territory of Belgium with the Netherlands to form a Kingdom of the Netherlands. In this arrangement, the Dutch were compensated for the British takeover of colonies in

Ceylon and the Cape of Good Hope. By the Congress's terms, in 1815, 39 German principalities were corralled into the German Confederation. However, it was difficult to uphold political legitimacy when, in the Netherlands, the Belgians were governed by the Dutch king William I and the House of Orange.

Restoring the House of Bourbon in France was more in step with Metternich's regard for, and understanding of, legitimacy. Over loud British objections, Bourbon control was reestablished in Spain and Naples. King Ferdinand I was placed on the throne of the Kingdom of the Two Sicilies in southern Italy and his nephew, Ferdinand VII, became the king of Spain. The only native ruler in Italy was the conservative Victor Emmanuel I, from the House of Savoy in the Kingdom of Piedmont (or Piedmont-Sardinia). His hand was strengthened when he acquired nearby Genoa. Later, in the 1840s and 1850s, he and his kingdom were instrumental

A production of the medieval Carousel and Knight's Pageant at the 1814 Congress of Vienna. Internal squabbling among the heads of state, particularly with Alexander I, temporarily turned Metternich's attention toward the social events of the Congress.

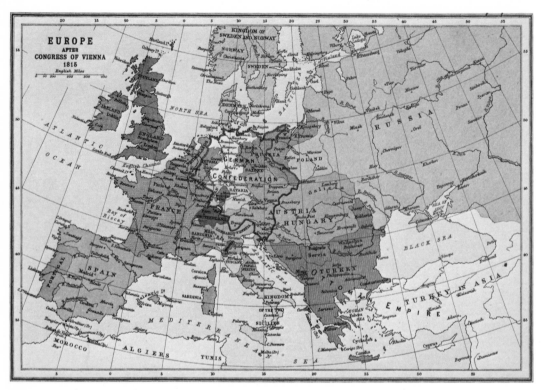

EUROPE
AFTER
CONGRESS OF VIENNA
1815
English Miles

Territorial controls in Europe were rearranged after the overthrow of Napoleon and the closing of the Congress of Vienna in 1815.

in unifying the Italian states against Austrian resistance.

Metternich had wanted to see an Italian confederation along the lines established in the German states. The settlement, as it happened, seemed to agree with Metternich. To him, Italy remained a "geographical expression," and Austria dominated in the affairs of the Italian peninsula, with the Archdukes of Habsburg governing in Modena and Tuscany. Marie Louise, daughter of Francis and consort of Napoleon, received compensation as the duchess of Parma. Catholic Austria was also on good terms with the Papal States and, thus, not a single area of Italy was out of touch with Austrian influence.

In addition to these many complex political adjustments there was the tsar's own diplomatic initiative, the Holy Alliance. The Holy Alliance expressed Alexander's faith in the precepts of Christian brotherhood. Alexander staunchly maintained that mutual understanding based on Christian doctrine was superior to mere contracts written by competing nations. Signed to appease the tsar on September 26, 1815, the Holy Alliance was dismissed by Castlereagh as a "piece of sublime mysticism and nonsense." Frederick William III of Prussia was its only supporter other than the passionate tsar himself. To Metternich it was a "loud-sounding nothing."

What mattered most at this point was that neither Castlereagh nor Metternich wanted to jeopardize the unity of the Coalition, for which the ground had been laid by the Treaty of Chaumont. They also did not want prospects for a Concert of Europe to be endangered by the Holy Alliance's abstract tone. Gentz called the Concert "the principle of a general union." A few small changes made by Metternich's pen, and the gap in the tsar's Alliance between idealism and practicality was bridged. The Holy Alliance was signed — not without hesitation — by the monarchs of Russia, Prussia, and Austria. Francis remained wary of Alexander's religious fervor but Metternich convinced the emperor to cooperate. Eventually, only Great Britain's reigning monarch refused to sign it. Other sovereigns whose signatures were absent from the document were the pope, who needed no instructions from the tsar on Christian doctrine, and the Turkish sultan, who was a Muslim. Its later importance to the balance of power was due to its having been signed at all, rather than its content, which asserted that "holy religion, precepts of justice, charity and peace. . . must. . . directly influence the decisions of princes."

For the moment, the Holy Alliance maintained the cooperation agreed upon at Chaumont and paved the way for the continuation of the Quadruple Alliance. Made along with the Second Peace of Paris (signed November 20, 1815) the Quadruple Alliance called on the four victors of the Napoleonic Wars to guarantee that the ensuing Restoration furthered European peace and prosperity. Austria, Great Britain, Prussia, and Russia pledged to act jointly if France should become aggressive once more, or if Napoleon should return. They concurred that they

Victor Emmanuel I, king of Sardinia, was the only native ruler in Italy after the Congress of Vienna. A reactionary ruler, he was eventually forced to abdicate his throne.

would cooperate in stamping out another revolution there as well. Furthermore, they agreed to hold periodic meetings regarding issues of mutual concern in the future, and proceeded, after 1818, to hold four such meetings. Thus was born the idea of the Concert of Europe. Conceived by Castlereagh, it became the most important vehicle for Metternich's furthering the Congress of Vienna. At first these meetings primarily dealt with France, then increasingly with revolutionary flare-ups in Europe and in the colonial possessions of Spain and Portugal. In reaction, British policy began to drift. Castlereagh firmly opposed interfering in the policies of other nations.

When France was admitted to the alliance system at the Congress of Aix-la-Chapelle in 1818, the Quadruple Alliance became the Quintuple Alliance and the balance of power that was established when Talleyrand joined the negotiations at the Congress of Vienna was reaffirmed. Metternich commented at Aix-la-Chapelle that he "never saw a prettier little congress. . . . Everything is wonderfully arranged. It will do us credit." For now, the Congress System that Metternich was trying to install was the same as Castlereagh's Concert of Europe. The first peacetime meeting over matters of mutual interest was, in fact, the Congress that met at the German town of Aix-la-Chapelle.

The Final Act, signed on June 9, 1815, had concluded Congress of Vienna and redistributed territory in accordance with the Big Four's wishes and transformed "compensation" and "legitimacy" into practical policy. Not until June 18 did Napoleon's lackluster tactics at Waterloo fail to overwhelm the duke of Wellington, after Marshal Blücher arrived in the nick of time with Prussian reinforcements. In October, after abdicating the throne for the last time, on June 22, Napoleon went into final exile off the African coast, on the island of St. Helena. Having secured peace in Europe, it was now most important for Metternich to maintain unity of purpose in the Habsburg holdings. This was the point at which cracks in Metternich's system were first revealed.

After Metternich's policies triumphantly culminated in the Battle of the Nations at Leipzig in 1813, he had been granted the title of prince by Francis. Although his father had failed in organizing a people's war in Belgium in 1793, Metternich had successfully harnessed the Prussian War of Liberation to imperial purposes at Leipzig and was rewarded. By 1818, the year of his father's death, however, Metternich was troubled by the continuing surge of nationalism found in the German universities, especially in Protestant institutions, and among the middle-class merchants in the German Confederation. Youthful idealism, liberal doctrines, and the desire of the middle classes for increased freedom combined to challenge Habsburg dominance over the confederation. The center of German nationalism was Prussia, and Metternich was quick to realize the threat to the existing balance of power and to the status quo. Stimulated by the patriotic youth organization called the *Tugendbund* in 1808, German nationalism was inspired by the Prussian philosopher Johann Gottlieb Fichte, the author in 1807 of *Reden an die Deutsche Nation* (*Speeches on the German Nation*).

Five years earlier, flexibility and practicality had been Metternich's keys to extraordinary diplomatic success. Inflexibility would now begin his gradual undoing. At the very moment when the spirit of cooperation seemed to be accomplished in European affairs, he introduced a policy of rigid repression in the German Confederation. To Metternich, it seemed calm should now prevail in Europe as part of the Restoration; political ferment in the German-speaking world, controlled by the Habsburgs, must be the result of lingering French radicalism.

The pretext for imposing this policy was the murder of the dramatist and writer August von Kotzebue by a nationalist student at the Protestant University of Jena. Strangely, it was the press that Metternich would seek to curb. At Teplitz in August of 1819, he met with Frederick William and Hardenberg, the foreign minister, and convinced the Prussian king that revolution was a serious danger in his realm.

Now that the balance of power and the sanctity of international agreements had become a matter of principle, Metternich was faced with the task of enforcement. Representatives from the leading German states then met at Carlsbad and agreed upon the measures authored by Metternich. The Carlsbad Decrees were aimed at controlling student unrest in the universities and establishing press censorship. Books, newspapers, and the theater were to be censored. Various academic studies were curtailed. Government spies were sent to attend university lectures to control both professors and students. Student societies were abolished, and study in foreign universities prohibited, as were the appointments of foreign professors. When the British press criticized Metternich for placing restrictions on newspapers, he retorted that *The Times* of London must be subversive. Castlereagh personally approved of Metternich's crackdown on press and academic freedom, but British public opinion did not smile on such a policy. British disenchantment increased with the prince's foreign and domestic policies. No Austrians were allowed to travel in foreign countries without a special permit. An elaborate police network to monitor political activity was placed under the jurisdiction of the Austrian foreign office. Metternich intended to keep control of political affairs throughout the German Confederation while Austria remained paramount among its members. These measures were submitted to the Diet of Frankfurt, accepted for a period of five years, and subject to renewal at the end of that period. To support these policies, another conference was held in Vienna in November 1819, to reinforce the measures taken at Carlsbad. Five years later the decrees were renewed among the German states in negotiations at Frankfurt.

It was Metternich who exerted real power over the German Confederation, as the most influential of Austrian statesmen. Still he had to meet threats to the status quo — revolutions against Bourbon rule in Spain and in Naples that were beyond the scope of the German Diet in Frankfurt. It was here that "the great machine of European safety," as Castlereagh called the Concert of Europe, began to falter. Castlereagh had miscalculated in thinking that peace and order would last. Europe was seething with movements eager to upset the prevailing peace and order. The Holy Alliance replaced the Concert of Europe as the scaffolding that held up the Congress System. During the 1820s, uprisings in Naples, in Spain and Portugal, in Piedmont, and in Greece, made this increasingly clear. National interests gradually replaced the spirit of common security envisioned at the Congress of Vienna, and Metternich had little choice but to revise his ap-

Following Castlereagh's suicide in August 1822, George Canning was appointed Britain's foreign minister. He refused to support Metternich's suppression of the popular uprisings occurring in other European nations.

After his final defeat at Waterloo in June 1815, Napoleon was exiled to the British island of Saint Helena, off the coast of Africa. He died there of cancer on May 5, 1821.

proach to the developing realities. Austria's demands for security made it align itself closely with the conservative outlooks of Russia and Prussia. Metternich was obliged to state his position in terms of rigid policies that he could not maintain alone. He was able to draw upon the Holy Alliance as a way to gain leverage.

The Congress of Troppau was convened in Austrian Silesia by Alexander in October 1820 to deal with the rebellions against the Bourbon restoration in Spain and the Kingdom of the Two Sicilies. No agreement was reached concerning either Spain or Naples. Significantly, a proclamation was signed by Russia, Prussia, and Austria, the three Great Powers, stating that, under the Holy Alliance, they could intervene at any time to bring smaller states back to the Great Alliance. Great Britain decried this policy agreement. When Britain and France refused to sign, united action was impossible and the Concert of Europe became an unworkable ideal. Behind this agreement, the *Protocole Préliminaire*, stood Klemens von Metternich.

Metternich used the tsar's Holy Alliance to uphold the solidarity of the eastern monarchies. This principle grew stronger and remained associated with the Holy Alliance. The Congress of Troppau was succeeded by the Congress of Laibach, which convened in January 1821. It sanctioned the use of Austrian troops in both Naples and in Piedmont to combat the rebels known as *Carbonari*. Metternich was now as free to intervene in Italian affairs as he had been earlier in the German states. Francis was so impressed with these achievements that Metternich was promoted to chancellor on May 25, 1821. This meant that Metternich's already extensive influence over domestic matters was increased, but his grip on foreign affairs was now diminished. Within the empire, Francis I felt more confident and exercised more control. Metternich's decision-making capabilities were then hindered at a time when they were certainly needed. Although politics continued to depend upon the art of compromise, the emperor's stubbornness made it even more difficult for his chancellor to choose to be flexible. Castlereagh's suicide on August 12, 1822, also contributed to a weaker bargaining position for the new chancellor. Castlereagh's successor, George Canning, was much more forceful in opposing the Austrian prerogative to send troops around Europe to put down popular revolts. As for the once feared general and emperor, later called simply "General Bonaparte" by his British captors, Napoleon died on May 5, 1821, on the island of St. Helena.

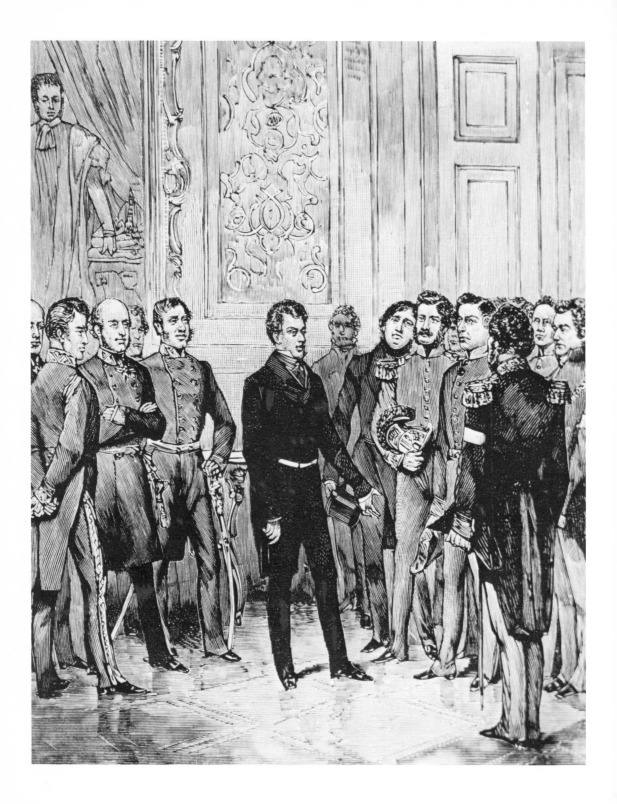

7

The Fortress Assailed

The Congress of Verona was held from October to December 1822. Metternich soon found himself in awkward circumstances at this conference. Tsar Alexander insisted on calling for intervention in Spain — though he was consulted originally to discuss the crisis that had broken out in Greece. Britain, as expected, opposed Russian intervention in Spain. Metternich had no desire to support Russian troops in Spain. He, nevertheless, was obliged to defend the legitimacy of the Bourbon monarchy. The compromise that was reached called for a French army to defend the Spanish Bourbons in the name of the Holy Alliance. The Quintuple Alliance was at an end and Metternich realized that his dependence on cooperation with Russia was vital to the preservation of the Congress System. When Alexander I died in December 1825, his antiprogressive successor, Nicholas I, further complicated Metternich's position. By 1826 he proved to have seriously misjudged the international climate.

When the Greek War of Independence broke out in 1821, led by the nationalist organization *Philike Hetairia*, Austria's dilemma was made clearer. The Congress of Verona had decided that the insurrection of the Greeks was a matter for the Turkish sultan to control. It was not a matter of upholding legitimacy by the Christian states of Europe until

Posterity will judge me. Her voice is the only one whose favors I seek, the only one to which I do not remain indifferent, and yet it is the only one I shall never hear.
—PRINCE METTERNICH

In 1848 Chancellor Metternich, whose ideals rested with the rapidly disintegrating system of imperial control, was forced to resign.

Nicholas I (1796–1855) succeeded Alexander I as tsar of Russia in 1825. On his first day as ruler, Nicholas crushed the revolutionary Decembrists, a liberal group.

Russia came to the support of the Greek Christians. Metternich supported the legitimacy of the Turkish sultan and hoped that the other European powers would cooperate and agree on this matter. He was able to convince Alexander that legitimacy in the Balkan region was as valid as in the rest of Europe, but Nicholas was determined to further Russian national interests. So were Great Britain and France. Russian support ensured that Greek independence fighters would accomplish their objective. In 1829, by the Treaty of Adrianople, Greece was established as an independent kingdom. Formal recognition came in 1832. Russia, France, and Britain had indeed worked in concert by sending warships to the area in 1827 to obtain a cease-fire and secure Greek independence. Suddenly, several leading powers had strayed from Metternich's definition of legitimacy. National interests were now widely becoming more important in Europe than the protection of the status quo. Contrary to the view Metternich tried to promote concerning the danger the fight for independence posed to European stability and safety, the world looked favorably upon the Greek struggle.

As Metternich observed international relations stray from his system he also endured a number of personal losses. That he succumbed to neither his political nor his personal misfortunes at this time is a tribute to his stamina and fortitude. Eleonore, his wife for almost 30 years, died on March 19, 1825. In spite of his numerous affairs with other women, Metternich had loved her dearly. They had six children and also raised Clementine, Metternich's child born out of wedlock. Two of these children had not survived their first year, including his namesake, Klemens. Two daughters died of tuberculosis in 1820; the 16-year-old Clementine died in May and Marie, the eldest daughter, in July, five days after Metternich learned of the revolution in Naples. He was still grieving upon his arrival at Troppau for the congress there in October 1820. Metternich loved his family, and it was common knowledge that his wife and children returned his affection. He missed the family life-style, and there was little surprise when Metternich married Marie-Antoinette von Leykam in November 1827. They had been married more than a year when Metternich's mother died. She did not live to see her new grandson, Richard, the future editor of his father's memoirs, who was born on January 7, 1829. Within 10 days of the delivery, Metternich's second wife also died. On November 30 of that year, his oldest son, Victor, died of tuberculosis.

In July 1830 he was greeted with the news of a revolution in Paris that overthrew the Bourbon monarchy and led to growing political unrest in Italy and Germany. There would be no rest for the troubled chancellor. Nevertheless, on January 30, 1831, Metternich was married again, this time to Mélanie Zichy-Ferraris, and the union lasted for more than 23 years. Four more children entered the family between 1832 and 1837, but a second son named Klemens, born in 1833, did not survive the year of his

The Greek war of independence freed the country from the Ottoman empire, which had dominated Greece since the mid-15th century, and established a constitutional monarchy.

birth. A year that yielded successes for Metternich in foreign policy brought sadness to his family.

The Congress System remained under the threat of rebellion in Germany, Italy, and Poland. Though the desire to gain constitutional government was a motive in these revolutions, they were fueled by the rising nationalist aspirations of Germans, Italians, and nationalists in opposition to Habsburg domination. Greeks struggled against Turks, Poles rose up against Russians, and the Belgians against the Dutch. The Magyar nationalist Lajos Kossuth eloquently demanded Hungarian independence, and students and workers petitioned for a constitutional assembly and individual rights.

Before long there came an even bigger shock in France. Louis XVIII died in 1824 and was succeeded

Lajos Kossuth, the dynamic Hungarian revolutionary, led his country in an uprising against Habsburg domination. The revolution of 1848 established an independent Hungarian nation under Kossuth.

Horace Vernet's painting depicts Charles X, who succeeded his brother Louis XVIII as king of France in 1824. His reactionary and repressive leadership further fueled liberal unrest.

by the ultraconservative count of Artois, who became Charles X. Charles's rule disintegrated when he used repressive measures, and in July 1830 students and workers rioted in the streets of Paris. On the night of July 27 barricades were erected. The City Hall in Paris was captured the following day, and a republic was proclaimed. Declared the intended president of the republic was Marquis Marie-Joseph de Lafayette, long a prominent and controversial figure of the French Revolution. After three days of fighting finally ended Bourbon rule in France, Charles X fled to Scotland.

In the confusion, a few wealthy bankers, headed by Talleyrand, the man Metternich considered "intended for destructive purposes," persuaded republicans in the City Hall that Louis Philippe, the duke of Orléans, was a more suitable ruler. When Lafayette agreed to this compromise, France became a constitutional monarchy rather than a republic. But this monarchy represented an important transition. It was called the bourgeois monarchy. Louis Philippe, the so-called bourgeois (or middle-class) king, was said to rule by the grace of God and the will of the people. His accession to the throne irreparably changed legitimacy as Metternich had worked to have it understood. It also made Metternich more distrustful of France. Talleyrand, too, had seen that this compromise was an unexpected turn of events. Governing power went to bankers, merchants, and manufacturers, not to the nobility. The Bourbon Restoration had been a keystone in upholding the principle of legitimacy, and France had been a vital link in the Concert of Europe ever since the Congress of Châtillon. That was now changed.

The Poles were brutally suppressed by Russia under Nicholas, but the Belgians freed themselves from the Dutch and Metternich was obliged to accept the results: Two years after their revolt in 1830,

The liberal French middle class opposed an attempt by Charles X to return to the *ancien régime*. In the 1830 "July Revolution" they stormed the city hall in Paris, overthrew Charles X, and established a French republic. Charles X died in exile.

the Belgians were made formally independent from the Dutch. Without a sufficient military force in Austria and without a secure coalition, principles gave way to realities. Metternich could now do little more than watch the old order crumble. The worst blow of all was the revolution in France. Summoned to attend the prince, Metternich's physician found him head in hands, moaning, "My whole life's work is destroyed."

Revolutionary fervor throughout Europe served to push Metternich again to the political forefront. No longer able to rely upon either Britain or France, Metternich was forced toward Russia and Prussia. A revolt by the Polish Cadets in Warsaw in November 1830 also made the tsar alert to a danger that Metternich well understood. National revolutions in Central Europe set off a panic that revived the notion of solidarity among monarchs, and Metternich used his influence to give it better form. His efforts led to Francis meeting with Nicholas and to a renewal of the Holy Alliance, when a pact was signed at Münchengrätz between Austria and Russia in September 1833. In Metternich's last significant contribution to the Congress System, the Berlin Convention reaffirmed the principle of intervention, and when Prussia approved, the three eastern powers were once more prepared to act in concert. European diplomacy was again set to squash threats to the dynastic order. Yet, the age of nationalism had begun, and the middle and working classes were playing an ever increasing role in it.

When Metternich celebrated his 65th birthday in 1838, he would be together with six surviving children, three of them under the age of six, but this was no measure of the tragedies through which the aging chancellor had passed. In addition to the death of several family members, his trusted friend and adviser, Friedrich von Gentz, died in 1832, and his emperor Francis, in March 1835. Metternich's task under the emperor had never been easy, but the two men understood and respected each other, having worked closely together since 1809. The statesman once wrote to a countess who admired

My most secret conviction is that the old Europe is nearing its end. I have determined to fall with it, and I shall know how to do my duty.
—PRINCE METTERNICH
in 1830

101

Marie-Joseph de Lafayette, French general and statesman, led the moderates in the "July Revolution" and was proclaimed president of the new French republic. Lafayette created the modern French flag.

him that "The Emperor always does what I want, but I never want him to do anything that he ought not to do." The emperor left a letter to his son Ferdinand I, the successor to the Habsburg throne, which began: "Disturb nothing in the foundations of the state. Govern, and change nothing." Ferdinand was hardly capable of more than this and was subject to fits of insanity. If the chancellor's role under Francis had been difficult, it was then worse. He had to serve as a governing regent for another 13 years because of Ferdinand's incapability.

His last accomplishment was the founding of the Vienna Academy of Sciences in January 1846. Otherwise, the final two years in office were full of foreboding. Many of the coming events of 1848 were predictable, and Metternich wrote in October, 1847: "I am an old doctor. I can distinguish a passing illness from a mortal ailment." Five months later he was faced with the demand for his own resignation.

Once more, Metternich's life was tied to events in France. For the third time in his life, he would see revolution kindled in Paris and its flames catch throughout Europe. For the second time, a French revolution would produce another Napoleon — Napoleon III. The first French Revolution and the wars that followed swept Metternich into politics. He weathered the revolutions of 1830, but the February Revolution of 1848 in Paris would bring about his

Louis Philippe (center) signs an 1830 proclamation that made him Lieutenant General. He quickly replaced Lafayette as ruler of France and established a constitutional monarchy. Louis was known as the "bourgeois king" because of his middle-class dress and manner.

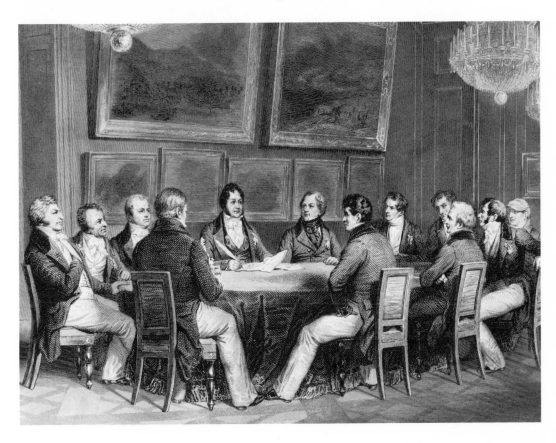

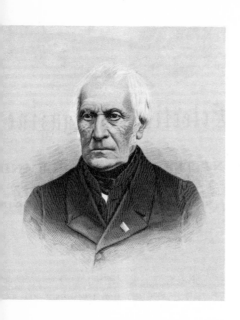

François Guizot, French statesman and university professor, was appointed prime minister in 1847, under King Louis Philippe. Because of his conservative politics, Guizot was forced to resign during the 1848 February Revolution, one day before the king abdicated.

collapse. As an opponent of Napoleon I he had been patient. During that contest time had been on his side; now it was turning against him. For 30 years the Congress System had been gradually withering away. It would, in part, survive beyond 1848, but without Metternich at the reins.

He had not been caught unaware. As early as 1821, Metternich had recognized his plight. "I feel in the midst of a web, like my friends the spiders, whom I love because I have so often wondered at them. . . . Such webs are pretty to look at, cleverly spun, and will bear a light touch but not a gale of wind." Metternich's musings became prophetic in March 1848 when his web was shattered by the gale winds of revolution. Developments not to his liking commenced in the summer of 1847. A number of French reformers, led by Adolphe Thiers, organized a series of banquets designed to force the resignation of the conservative prime minister, François Guizot. One of these banquets was scheduled for February 22, 1848, in honor of George Washington's birthday. The banquet was banned by Guizot and this action increased the existing political unrest. On the day of the scheduled banquet, demonstrations broke out in the streets of Paris. From these demonstrations came a violent wave of revolutionary activity that threatened to overthrow governments from Berlin to Rome, from Paris to Vienna. The following day, Guizot was forced to resign by Louis-Philippe, who abdicated the following day, February 24. In June, armed Parisian workers, many of them inspired by socialist thought, armed Parisian workers manned makeshift barricades. The insurrection was suppressed by the army under the provisional government after three days of bloody fighting in the streets. In December Louis Napoleon Bonaparte, nephew of Napoleon, was elected president of the Second French Republic. Within three years, he had undermined the Second Republic and was proclaimed Emperor Napoleon III by a plebiscite on December 1, 1852. The nightmare of the Congress of Vienna had been realized, for the plebiscite also turned the French republic into another Bonapartist empire.

From the beginning, Metternich's career was tied to the larger patterns of European history, and so it was at the end. He had chosen to uphold a conservative position based upon the legitimacy of monarchical principles. This position became increasingly untenable.

Successive problems both within and beyond the confines of the Austrian Empire had been met with his resolve. The disturbances of 1830 to his international system had been surmounted, but the events in Paris had driven Metternich to the brink of despair. He collapsed at his desk when reports of the July Revolution reached him. That reaction was overstated and premature. France did receive a new constitution, and with it, a new king. Both the French monarchy and Metternich remained in power for another 18 years. Late in the year 1822, Metternich foresaw his future predicament, and his diagnosis was even truer in 1848: "My life has coincided with an abominable time. I came into the world too soon or too late. . . . I spend my time shoring up crumbling edifices. I should have been born in 1900 with the twentieth century before me."

In 1848, the "crumbling edifices" could be shored up no longer, but the chancellor remained at his post. His personal convictions again led him toward vigorous suppression of any upheaval in the streets.

This time, however, the old unity of the past was absent. Metternich knew that he had powerful enemies at court, but he did not seem to realize how much the Empire had changed. His sense of imperial tradition was conservative; the growing sense of national traditions was revolutionary. Economic changes wrought by the Industrial Revolution created a new working class that combined with militant national movements. The combination produced the "monstrous brew," Metternich dreaded. A mob of students, workers, and nationalists demanded Metternich's resignation. The elderly master of diplomacy, then 75 years old, was now the cause of violent student unrest in Vienna. In Paris, Guizot had already been dismissed in February 1848. On March 13 it was Metternich's turn. A committee of archdukes, representing the em-

After the February Revolution, Napoleon III, nephew of Napoleon I, was elected president of the second French republic, but within four years he established himself as emperor of France. He was finally deposed in September 1870, during the Franco-Prussian War.

By 1848, Metternich had fallen out of favor with the Austrian people; this caricature depicts his flight from his homeland. He was exiled to London and two years later moved to Brussels.

peror, asking for Metternich's resignation, hoped to appease the revolutionaries. To avert further disorder the venerable chancellor had to accept his responsibility. The coachman of Europe went into exile in London. Two years later he moved to Brussels. Though he returned to Vienna in 1851, he never held office again.

The provisions that were established by the Congress of Vienna prevented a general European war for an entire century, but the system in the German states by 1819, in Italy and Spain in 1820, France in 1830, and most of western Europe by 1848 had come apart. The revolutions that produced Napoleon III led to the unification of Italy in 1861, and Germany in 1870. By then, the verdict had long been in regarding the durability of Metternich's Europe. The era of the Prussian statesman Otto von Bismarck was replacing the age of Metternich. On June 4, 1859, in the wars of Italian unification, the Austrian army was defeated at the Battle of Magenta. One week later, Metternich was dead.

One question dogged Metternich's later years: How could the dynastic and aristocratic government survive amid emerging democracies, nationalism, and industrial economies? Metternich's answer was to preserve the old world by restraining the new forces. This conservatism guided Metternich's actions and thinking after the defeat of Napoleon. His growing inflexibility was partly the result of such a task. He did not have the means at his disposal to maintain his design, but this recognition does not mean that Metternich failed to understand the conflicts around him. In many of his writings, he acknowledged that the world was in flux, that it was changing. But this meant that what he most desired to preserve was bound to slip away. Thus, he concluded that the civilization, as he knew it, was declining. Never truly a man of the 19th century, Metternich remained loyal to his aristocratic origins. Never doubting the correctness of his own actions, Metternich was the architect of a foreign policy that aimed at balancing one nation's interests

Metternich returned to Vienna in 1852 but never again held office. The world he had worked to establish during the 1814 Congress of Vienna was crumbling, and the imperialistic "Age of Metternich" was near its end.

against another. His domestic policies, however, depended on repression. The "Age of Metternich" was hostile to freedom. By placing liberty and national independence out of reach of subject peoples, Metternich's own rigid methods helped bring about the revolutions he so much wanted to prevent. Seeing only within the parameters of his aristocratic perspective, Metternich decided that European civilization had reached its peak. His vision of the future demanded that society remain unchanged. No advances could be made without damaging a delicate society, a precarious balance.

At the same time, he belonged, he wrote, "to the class of men who live more in the future than in the present." The Austrian Empire survived for another 70 years following Metternich's resignation, until it provided the spark that ignited World War I, in which the empire was finally destroyed.

Further Reading

Kissinger, Henry A. *A World Restored, Europe after Napoleon: The Politics of Conservatism in a Revolutionary Age.* New York: Grosset and Dunlap, 1964.

May, Arthur J. *The Age of Metternich, 1814–1848.* New York: Holt, Rinehart and Winston, 1963.

Metternich, Prince Richard, ed. *Memoirs of Prince Metternich, Vols. I–IV.* New York: Howard Fertig, 1970.

Milne, Andrew. *Metternich.* Totowa, NJ: Rowan and Littlefield, 1975.

Palmer, Alan. *Metternich.* New York: Harper & Row, 1972.

Viereck, Peter. *Conservatism Revisited: The Revolt Against Revolt, 1815–1949.* London: John Lehman Ltd., 1950.

Ward, David. *1848: The Fall of Metternich and the Year of Revolution.* New York: Weybright and Talley, 1970.

Woodward, E. L. *Three Studies in European Conservatism. Metternich: Guizot: The Catholic Church in the Nineteenth Century.* London: Frank Cass and Co., Ltd., 1963.

Chronology

May 15, 1773	Klemens von Metternich born in Koblenz
1788	Enters the University at Strasbourg
1789	French Revolution begins
1790	Metternich studies law at University of Mainz
July 1792	Coronation of Emperor Francis II in Frankfurt
1797	Metternich begins political career as Westphalian College of Counts' Representative at the Congress of Rastatt
Nov. 1799	Napoleon gains power via successful coup d'état
1801	Metternich enters diplomatic service at the Court of Saxony
1803	Becomes Austrian Ambassador in Berlin
Dec. 1805	Austria and allies defeated by Napoleon at Austerlitz
May 1806	Metternich becomes Ambassador to France
Aug. 1806	Holy Roman Empire comes to an end
1809–1810	Metternich appointed Minister of Foreign Affairs for the Austrian Empire
Aug. 10, 1813	Austria declares war on France
Oct. 18, 1813	Napoleon defeated at Battle of the Nations at Leipzig
Oct. 20, 1813	Metternich receives title of prince
Sept. 1814	Presides over opening of the Congress of Vienna
Jun. 18, 1815	Battle of Waterloo, Napoleon's final defeat
1818	Congress of Aix-la-Chapelle
1819	Carlsbad Decrees
1820	Congress of Troppau Italian revolts are suppressed
May 5, 1821	Napoleon dies
May 25, 1821	Metternich named chancellor of Austrian Empire
1822	Congress of Verona
1827	London Conference on Greek Affairs leading to Treaty of London
1830	King Charles X overthrown; King Louis Philippe and the July Monarchy seize power in France
1832	Diet of Frankfurt passes decrees curbing civil liberties
Oct. 15, 1833	Berlin Convention and alliance between the three eastern monarchies
1840	Metternich begins work on his memoirs
Jan. 1846	Founds the Vienna Academy of Sciences
Feb. 1848	Revolution in Paris; revolution sparked throughout Europe
March 13, 1848	Riots in Vienna force Metternich to resign and flee the city
Sept. 24, 1851	Returns to Vienna
Dec. 1852	Louis Napoleon becomes Emperor Napoleon III of France
Jun. 11, 1859	Metternich dies in Vienna

Index

John von der Heide is Kenan Professor of History and chairman of the history department at Drew University. He received the Ph.D. degree from Northwestern University in 1963, specializing in 19th-century European history. He is a father of two, an avid sports fan, and an amateur jazz pianist.

Arthur M. Schlesinger, jr., taught history at Harvard for many years and is currently Albert Schweitzer Professor of the Humanities at City University of New York. He is the author of numerous highly praised works in American history and has twice been awarded the Pulitzer Prize. He served in the White House as special assistant to Presidents Kennedy and Johnson.

PICTURE CREDITS

Bibliotheque Nationale: p. 107; Culver Pictures: pp. 2, 24, 26, 42; The Bettmann Archive: pp. 12, 14, 15, 16, 17, 18, 19, 20, 21, 22, 23, 26, 28, 30, 31, 32, 33, 34, 35, 36, 38, 40, 41, 43, 45, 46, 47, 48, 49, 50, 52, 53, 54, 55, 56, 57, 59, 60, 62, 63, 64, 67, 69, 70, 72, 74, 77, 78, 80, 82, 85, 86, 87, 91, 92, 94, 96, 97, 98, 99, 100, 102, 103, 104, 105, 106